1

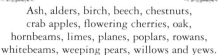

SOMERSET VOICES
A Celebration of Memories

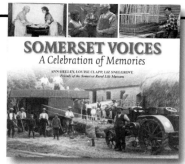

This fascinating book, illustrated in colour
and black & white throughout, is drawn from the
collection of over six hundred oral recordings of
Somerset people made since 1973 and held
at the Somerset Rural Life Museum.

Life is shown as it really was in the twentieth century. It features memories of childhood,
everyday tasks, social life, manual work and the joys of mechanization, cider making and
cheese making, war time changes, peat digging and much more.

Those interviewed came from across the County including west Somerset, the Quantock
villages, the Levels and the Moors, the coast, central and south Somerset and the Mendip Hills.

£14.99, 978 0 86183 447 1, hardback, 144 pages   *Somerset Books*

A SMALL SELECTION OF HALSGROVE' SUPERB BOOKS* COVERING EXMOOR AND WEST SOMERSET

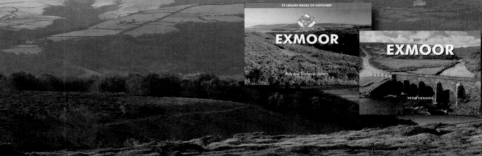

NEW
West Somerset in the News
£19.99, Jeff Cox, hardback, 160 pages

NEW
The Overland Launch
£9.99, C. Walter Hodges, hardback, 112 pages

Exmoor – A Winter's Tale
£14.99, Neville Stanikk, hardback, 144 pages

NEW
Portrait of the Somerset Coast
£14.99, Neville Stanikk, hardback, 144 pages

Somerset Coast from the Air
£14.99, Jason Hawkes, hardback, 132 pages

NEW
The West Somerset Railway Revisited
£16.99, Don Bishop, hardback, 144 pages

Spirit of the West Somerset Railway
£4.99, Don Bishop, hardback, 64 pages

A Boot Up Exmoor
£4.99, Adrian Tierney-Jones, hardback, 64 pages

Watchet Reunited
£19.99, Maurice and Joyce Chidgey, hardback, 160 pages

Somerset – The Glorious County
£14.99, Tony Howell, hardback, 144 pages

An Exmoor Panorama
£24.99, Peter Hendrie, hardback, 144 pages

NEW
Spirit of Exmoor
£4.99, Peter Hendrie, hardback, 64 pages

Perfect Exmoor
£14.99, Neville Stanikk, hardback, 144 pages

Charles Wood's Somerset Quiz Book
£8.99, paperback, 96 pages

Exmoor Ponies – Survival of the Fittest: A Natural History
£19.99, Sue Baker, hardback, 256 pages

NEW
Exmoor Amour
£12.99, Charles Wood,
hardback, 168 pages

Surviving Another
Somerset Year
£12.99, Charles Wood,
hardback, 160 pages

How to
Survive in Somerset
£12.99, Charles Wood,
hardback, 160 pages

Norma Huxtable's
Exmoor Exposed
£4.99, hardback, 64 pages

The Spirit of
the Exmoor Pony
£4.99, Shanan and Lisa
Leigh, hardback, 64 pages

The Spirit of
Exmoor Red Deer
£4.99, Ray Stoneman,
hardback, 64 pages

Murder and Mystery
on Exmoor
£4.95, Jack Hurley,
paperback, 80 pages

A Moorland Year
£12.95, Hope Bourne,
hardback, 192 pages

Wild Harvest
£12.95, Hope Bourne,
hardback, 136 pages

The Old Mineral Line
£4.99, R J Sellick,
paperback, 64 pages

Growing Wild on Exmoor
£12.99, Molly Richards,
hardback, 96 pages

The Last Word on Exmoor
£12.99, Norma Huxtable,
hardback, 144 pages

Sir Antony Acland

EXMOOR

Infinite variety is part of the charm of Exmoor, for the landscape is a mixture of moorlands and vast views, precipitous and spectacular cliffs, deeply incised wooded combes, rolling hills, traditional upland farms and narrow lanes lined with beech hedges connecting picturesque villages, hamlets and farmsteads. A mosaic of habitats supports a great diversity of wildlife, including herds of wild red deer, rich lichen communities, rare fritillary butterflies, and bats. It is an historic landscape that provides a record of how people have lived here since the last ice age. All this is found in a relatively small area of 170,000 acres.

Exmoor's special qualities relate to its distinct landscape, wildlife and cultural heritage. In particular the large areas of open moorland provide a rare sense of remoteness, wildness and tranquillity. It is a farmed landscape with distinctive breeds and a rural community with strong farming traditions. With an exceptional rights of way network and extensive areas of access land it provides superb opportunities for walking, riding and cycling.

A landscape, then, that provides inspiration, livelihoods and prosperity for many but remains fragile and vulnerable to incremental change destroying its unique qualities.

THE EXMOOR SOCIETY

The Exmoor Society was formed in 1958 initially to protest about the proposed afforestation of the Chains and later to save the moorlands from ploughing and fencing. Although successful in these tasks, there are still threats to the moorland today but they are more complex and difficult to solve. There are also new pressures including climate change and its impact on wildlife; increasing recreational demands and development and the loss of rural services and little affordable housing.

We act as an independent champion and watchdog for Exmoor and encourage the understanding of the National Park's special qualities.

We promote responsible enjoyment and access and develop educational and other projects.

We support upland farming and the local economy and community and stimulate public debate on these matters and campaign for sustainable solutions

We issue free to members a Newsletter in March, an Annual Report in August and the Exmoor Review in October. Our reference library and archives are open to the public.

Join us and help protect Exmoor for all time – *see contact details on next page*

EDITORIAL

Welcome to the latest Exmoor Review – the first for a long time not to benefit from Brian Pearce's versatile skills. But it's a pleasure to celebrate him here.

As usual, we present a fascinating set of reflections, reports, analyses, reminiscences, ruminations and descriptions of many aspects of Exmoor. And some personal views too, which may challenge conventional thinking. The Society has never feared controversy.

This edition focuses on people. In the end, it all comes down to individuals: their unique qualities, their achievements, and the example they set. Pride of place goes to our President, in a special year. We thank Sir Antony for his leadership, which has guided us safely through many turbulences. Our obituaries commemorate three special people, each of whom made their own unique contribution. Historical people figure large. Hazel Eardley-Wilmot of course, along with the brave Colonel Maclaren and assorted wonderful characters from the past. Read here too about one of Exmoor's most intrepid defenders of today – Molly Groves. And Christina Williams, who struck unexpected but wholly justified gold at Chelsea.

Many remain unnamed – it was ever thus: those who quietly support projects like the Lynton and Barnstaple Railway, the survival of the Exmoor pony, and the farmers who maintain the National Park for all of us.

Exmoor of course is more than a special landscape. There are settlements – people again – which pose increasing problems. Ben Hamilton-Baillie's approach to Dunster has much to offer other towns and villages across Exmoor. And how we use the rivers needs sorting out…

We are pleased to present the winners' photos from our Alfred Vowles Competition, which include pictures of people at work – a crucial part of Exmoor.

We range then from road clutter to local papers, from starry skies to wind turbines, from new discoveries of ancient sites to innovative weapon technology, from historical characters to the feelings of a stag – Exmoor comprises all this, and so much more.

The challenge is not only to preserve and protect Exmoor, but also to share it with other people, especially the young – which the Mosaic Project described here addresses. We for our part will continue to do our best to work out how our National Park might evolve the better to address all this, as Rachel Thomas, Adrian Phillips, Nigel Stone and many of our other contributors show. Thankyou to all of them.

Enjoy this latest Review, and tell us what you think.

Richard Westcott, Editor

RIGHT: The Exmoor Society Christmas Card. 'Valley of Rocks' from an original by Barry Watkin FRSA.
8"x6"in packs of 10 at £5.00 plus £1.15 p&p. Cards can be collected from the Parish Rooms, Dulverton or ordered by post.

Contents

Cover picture: *Axe Ascends*, Tony Nicholson
Volume No. 52 ISBN 978 0 900131 72 1 © The Exmoor Society
Produced for the Exmoor Society by Halsgrove, Wellington, Somerset. Printed by SRP Ltd., Exeter

CRYING THE MOOR

An Exmoor Miscellany

MIKE SHERWIN

Happy Birthday!
On a sunny Sunday afternoon, 6th June, a motley group of Society members marked the 80th birthday of Sir Antony with a short walk to the Jubilee Hut near Webbers Post, where a plaque was unveiled to commemorate the occasion. Our President was as delighted as he was surprised. The happy occasion was rounded off by a splendid tea party at Piles Mill, generously hosted by the National Trust.

MIKE SHERWIN

Moorland Mousie
The Exmoor Pony Centre reports that they are now in the thick of the high season, entertaining and educating visitors about the wonderful qualities of the very special breed (considered at greater length later in this Review).

Once the snow cleared and life got back to some sort of normality, the Society's sponsored Exmoor pony, originally the prosaic H67/123, but now known to his friends as

Kickums, was waved off on the next part of his journey through life as a conservation grazer, following the usual pattern for the youngsters who come in to the Centre's care. It gives them a chance to grow on and develop social skills within a group, as well as continuing to interact with human company, as the are checked on daily by wardens and volunteers, who enjoy seeing them.

Kickums is presently on National Trust land at Woolacombe, high above the beach with spectacular sea views, sharing his land with 15 pony friends and a paragliding club who regularly use his site as a take-off and landing pad. It's amazing how used to these extraordinarily brightly-coloured craft the Exmoor ponies have become. Perhaps this experience helps accustom them to traffic at an early age – or at least to begin to understand a little the strange creatures that purport to help them... Unfortunately the bad weather brought the neutering programme to an abrupt halt, so his visit from the vet has been postponed until Autumn, at the earliest.

Some exciting news for Moorland Mousie fans is that the go ahead has been given from the Mary Wace and Lionel Edwards estates to reprint the book – a 21st Century MM has long been eagerly awaited. Publication dates and details will be released as soon as possible, but enquiries are welcome. The Centre very much looks forward to the little pony finding himself back in the best-sellers, a hundred years on.

If you would like to sponsor a pony, please contact the Trust at the Exmoor Pony Centre.

Val Sherwin, Founder

Chelsea Gold

The Two Moors Festival Garden, supported by the Exmoor and Dartmoor National Parks' Sustainable Development Funds, scooped a double at the Chelsea Flower Show - a Gold Medal and the award for Best Courtyard Garden in the Show. The garden had a Westcountry feel - through Gothic willow arches could be seen moorland in the distances, with a solitary hawthorn amongst Molinia grasses. There was granite from Dartmoor and cobbles from Exmoor and the garden lies in the lee of the church, with planting characteristic of the region. Designed to celebrate the tenth anniversary of The Two Moors Festival, the garden highlights the links between music, flowers, gardens and the open countryside. By drawing the elements together and involving the local community, Christina Williams, the garden's designer hoped to increase the awareness of the cultural qualities of the South West and inform people of the unique environment of the two moors. Read more about this wonderful achievement within.

The Impacts of
Small Wind Turbines on Exmoor

Due to the recent battles to prevent the erection of industrial scale wind turbines close to the borders of Exmoor, many people are aware of the impact that these can have on the landscape and those that live and work within it.

Now that the Government has introduced the Feed In Tariff to encourage small scale renewables it may be time to look at the impacts of domestic and farm-scale wind turbines. The new system has made these turbines a more attractive financial proposition and has caused much more interest in them. There is little doubt that there will be a substantial number of applications within the National Park.

Whilst many will support such applications as a means of producing renewable energy it is important to remember that, as with most technologies, there are downsides to these turbines. Such turbines are usually up to about 30 metres in height, and whilst they may have advantages in producing energy and producing an income for the owners, they can have disadvantages in terms of visual impact and noise.

By their very nature, wind turbines are usually sited on high ground which increases their visual impact and turbines of 30 metres or so can be highly intrusive. This means that they need to sympathetically sited, especially when in it is borne in mind that there are likely to be a substantial number proposed in the near future because of the new incentives. Whilst an individual turbine may not change the landscape character of an area, a substantial number of inappropriately sited turbines could well do so.

Exmoor has many open vistas that are free of man-made structures and a proliferation of small scale turbines on upland sites could damage the character of the National Park and may deter tourists. It is worth noting that the NPA "State of Tourism Report" of 2008 found that 93% of visitors came to Exmoor for the scenery and that 76% came for the tranquillity. If that scenery and tranquillity are compromised then the number of visitors may fall.

Another problem is the impact of noise if turbines are sited too close to dwellings or tourist attractions. Turbine noise can be invasive and annoying so care needs to be taken to ensure that turbines are sited to prevent noise nuisance.

Studying a number of applications for such turbines elsewhere in Devon and Somerset reveals that the applicants often do not provide sufficient information to allow planning authorities and consultees to make an informed judgement on the effects that the proposal may have. This has caused a number to be refused and sometimes appeals have been lodged. It is crucial in the case of any applications within the National Park that sufficient environmental information is submitted. This should include an assessment of the landscape impact, the visual impact and a proper noise assessment. By doing so the National Park Authority will be able to make a proper informed judgement in each case.

Bob Barfoot

Not so Lone Rangers

30th March saw the latest cohort of 33 Junior Exmoor Rangers graduate from the four year course at Dulverton Middle School. The ceremony was attended by sponsors of the course – The Exmoor Society represented by Chris Whinney, and The Exmoor National Park represented by Patrick Watts-Mabbot.

The students were delighted to receive recognition of their hard work in the form of a new Junior Ranger Sweatshirt and Exmoor Society Tie which will now distinguish them from the other pupils at the school. The course has three levels an experienced qualification, a pass qualification and a graduate qualification. This is the eighth successive year of the Exmoor Curriculum scheme, a now nationally recognised good example of local curriculum. The course develops local interests and study and uses the moor as an outside classroom. The students experience a great variety of activities ranging from hill walking, sailing, kayaking, to nature study, presentation skills and public speaking. The course makes education at Dulverton Middle School too good to miss!

Pictured are the new cohort of graduates with Assistant Head Clive Goulty, Chris Whinney of the Exmoor Society and Patrick Watts-Mabbot of Exmoor National Park.

Our very own salmon…

As part of the River Exe Project, supported by the Exmoor National Park Sustainable Development Fund, Dulverton Middle School, Exford Primary, Uplowman Primary and Blundells Preparatory School have been rearing their own River Exe Salmon in their classrooms. John Hickey, River Exe Project Officer from the Westcountry Rivers Trust, has been running the scheme with schools and undertook the first education visits to the schools last autumn. Through the visits the schools have been learning about the River Exe, its water cycle and its wildlife.

The salmon fry were released recently by the children from Dulverton and Exford into the Haddeo in an area of excellent habitat, which will offer them the best chance of survival. Although only about 3-4 centimetres long, each fish is at this stage independent so ready to fight for enough space in the stream to provide shelter between the stones and to find a good food supply to allow it to grow strongly, and develop into parr.

With luck, after two years in the nursery streams the juvenile salmon parr will have reached about 12-15 centimetres. Then they will smolt and emigrate to sea in the spring, to begin the migration to the rich feeding grounds off Greenland. This marine phase may last for two years before they return to complete the breeding cycle in the very areas where they were released by our school children, four years previously.

Planning Matters

The year started with the welcome news from the Planning Inspector that a proposal for 13 large scale wind turbines, on hills just to the south of the National Park boundary, would not be allowed.

The Public Inquiry for this proposal took place in June and July 2009. To fight the proposals the Exmoor Society formed a partnership with The Campaign to Protect Rural England (Devon) and the Two Moors Campaign, called the Rural Exmoor Alliance. Exmoor Society Members donated enough funds to help pay for evidence to be put forward at the Inquiry by a professional Landscape Architect on behalf of the Rural Exmoor Alliance.

The Planning Inspector's decision came through on 29th January 2010 and although the site is outside the boundary of the National Park, the Inspector accepted that the turbines would have an unacceptable impact on the setting of the Exmoor National Park and its beauty, character and special qualities.

During the past couple of years we have seen a number of applications coming forward for small scale wind turbines for domestic use within the National Park. The National Park's planning policy for small scale wind turbines is a presumption to permit where they are compatible with the conservation of the landscape and wildlife of the National Park. The Exmoor Society supports this policy and has supported well-sited schemes but has made comment or objected to proposals with unacceptable landscape impact.

Finally, an application by a local hotel for conversion back into a dwelling house, following a long period of unsuccessful marketing for sale as a hotel, has highlighted a policy which the Exmoor Society believes could be less rigid in exceptional circumstances. Within the National park any building converted to a dwelling house has to be for local needs housing and not for the open market. The Society agrees with the policy because there is a need for affordable housing within the Park. However, in this particular case we believe this hotel was unsuitable for conversion into several local needs houses/flats as its location is rather remote, not being in a village with public transport and other local facilities. Since the original application , the planners and the owners have reached a compromise where the property will be converted to a single open market dwelling with an annex which will be an affordable, local needs house. This shows that the planning system can be flexible in exceptional circumstances and praise must go to the planners for a sensible approach to this matter.

Julia Thomas-Everard

Exmoor Livestock Prices 2009/2010

It was in the 2009 Volume of the Review when we last looked at livestock prices – time for another look, though this is something that affects our farmers on a daily basis, and all those who eat, and love Exmoor and its environment. I say 'eat' because all foodstuffs are linked together in the human food web; no calves, no dairy cows, no cheese for example. And I also mention the environment because Exmoor looks the way it does because of the way that it has been farmed by men and women for thousands of years. Sorry to reiterate those points, but some people forget, or don't appreciate it in the first place. We can all sleep safe in our beds though in the knowledge that if the sheep were to go we could always replace them with robot grazers.

Anyway back to prices. At the major two day sale of busk calves (6 to 10 month old weaned calves from suckler cows) at Cutcombe last Autumn steer calves averaged £585 and heifers £506. Store lambs at Blackmoor Gate averaged £44 in mid October, rising to £52 at the end of November, £56 in December and £60 a piece in January 2010. Autumn 2009 saw a good trade for breeding ewes, and the first Monday of September saw 1500 ewes of all ages average £98, with the Exmoor Mule Shearlings (Bluefaced Leicester Ram on an Exmoor Horn ewe) averaging £111.

Of course if it hadn't been for the development of Exmoor Farmers Livestock Auctions, we might not have any Exmoor prices to report. It was formed in 1997, and is owned by approximately 180 – mainly farmer – shareholders throughout the area. The new development at Cutcombe reported in the last Exmoor Review (51, p.21), is now well under way, and it is Exmoor Farmers Livestock Auctions that run the livestock markets at Cutcombe and Blackmoor Gate.

Nationally beef prices are down on last year (have you noticed it in the shops?), though lamb prices were up until about April/May, when they fell in line with last year. Up, down, sideways, the fact still remains that farmers are not paid a fair return for their produce that allows them to live and invest for the future despite additional farm payments. This has been highlighted recently in the press and is also something that the Exmoor Society is concerned about particularly, as it affects our upland and hill areas (see the Spring 2010 Newsletter and the 2008-2009 Annual Report.) Don't be fooled by land prices, current figures in the press do not reflect the income potential for the land and have never really done so. If you have eaten today thank a farmer, and hopefully we will have a future without robot sheep grazing our hills.

Sean and Albert Beer

With grateful thanks to Peter Huntley (Exmoor Farmers Livestock Auctions www.exmoorfarmers.co.uk) and the *Farmer Guardian* 25/6/2010 for livestock prices. For more details on the Exmoor Mule go to www.exmoorhornbreeders.co.uk

Mosaic and Young Champions

A hot July Saturday in central Bristol, with loud reggae music, thumping sound systems, brightly costumed dancers and exotic food - doesn't sound like the kind of place you'd expect to find The Exmoor Society. But this was St Paul's Carnival, and two members of the Bristol Group helped out on a stall organised by The Mosaic Project. This is a campaign run by the National Parks to attract more visitors from Black & Minority Ethnic communities. Many people picked up leaflets and copies of the *Exmoor Visitor*, along with gifts for children and old postcards. There was certainly a diverse range of backgrounds and ages, with many stopping to chat and ask questions. It was encouraging to hear questions about cycling and public transport. One of the aims of Mosaic is to recruit local Community Champions who will engage in a two-way process of actively promoting the National Parks within their community and communicating the needs of the community back to the Park Authorities. The project runs until March 2012 and we have several ideas to improve the stall for next year.

David Sinden and Mike Wilkinson

Mosaic is described more fully inside this Review, and for more information see www.mosaicnationalparks.org.

'Young Champions' recruited from Barnstaple and Bideford have also been involved in a range of activities that will help them enthuse other young people to make the most of the many opportunities Exmoor offers. The Champions have also 'youth proofed' the National Park Centre at Dunster. They are currently helping the Interpretation Team with a pocket guide for young people and giving advice on how to make the Authority's website more young person friendly.

Exmoor Challenge

Dulverton Middle and Community School were once again delighted to host the Rotary Club "Exmoor Challenge" on Saturday 1st May. As always the school had a strong showing in the final results with one of our five submitted teams coming in 2nd. This annual event has become an excellent tradition of engaging young people with Exmoor and the environment. This year

over 500 young people took part in teams of 4 in the 16 mile challenge walk. The weather was kind and the event was another great success. Pictured are the 5 teams entered by the Middle School and their mentor for the event Mr Goulty.

Forest Schools

British Forest Schools have been developed from an original concept in Sweden in the 1950s. Now found throughout other Scandinavian and European countries. In the 1980s Denmark started pre-school or early year's education forest schools. In the 1990s nursery nurses from Somerset visited. Then other early years professionals visited too. Learning in an outdoor woodland environment. All ages of children in fact.

The little ones (aged 3-4) from St Dubricus School go once a week by minibus to a piece of woodland near Piles Mill which is loaned by the Holnicote Estate. They do various activities such as building bridges over streams, climbing trees, playing hide and seek, building shelters, etc. Then they all sit round a camp fire drinking hot chocolate and eating biscuits. When I went, every child seemed to be aiming to get as muddy as possible, which wasn't difficult as it had rained a lot and the wood was very muddy!! They are intrepid and go in all weathers.

It is becoming increasingly recognised that the outdoor approach to play and learning can have a huge impact on the normal development of children.

A study in Sweden showed that children attending Forest School kindergartens in the countryside environment are far happier than those in an urban environment. They are more balanced, better at socialising and have fewer days off sick. They are more able to concentrate and have better co-ordination than city kindergarten children.

They felt the reasons for this were that nature presents a greater range of opportunities for play, and the children played for a longer time with less interruption by other children. When city children were interrupted they became irritable and stressed and couldn't concentrate, which made them more selfish and inconsiderate to other children. Their aggressive behaviour increased. The Forest School children were much more considerate towards each other.

The study also showed that the Forest School children had 25% fewer days off sick than the city children. This may be due to fresher air outside, and less chance of catching infections. The pleasant, natural, fun environment of the outdoors is less stressful, whereas stress impairs the immune system.

Children who had attended Forest School kindergartens (pre-school) were arriving at school with stronger social skills, greater ability to work in groups, and generally more confident in their own capabilities. This in turn raised academic achievement.

Dr Lesley Evans

EXMOOR PEOPLE

Sir Antony Acland

Sir Antony is a family man. Surrounded by pictures of his own family, it seemed only natural that he should tell us something about the distinguished history of the Aclands. It was in 1155 that Henry II granted land to an Acland – so called either because he took a Saxon Acca's land, or because he was a Flemish mercenary called Eccelin, and the name changed over the years to Akelane, and thence Acland – since when the line has continued.

The Aclands enjoyed two great talents. One was to generate male heirs in sufficient abundance to maintain the direct line through the centuries. The second was to marry women who brought large tracts of land into the family. The best example occurred in 1746 when Sir Thomas Acland married Elizabeth Dyke, who had herself inherited substantial estates, transferring Pixton Park, Tetton Park and Holnicote to the Aclands. The high water mark was reached around 1800, at which point some 56,000 acres stretching from Barnstaple to Minehead and down to Exeter prompted the myth that you could walk from the Bristol Channel to the English Channel, without leaving Acland land. Not actually true, said Sir Antony – though probably there was at least some land in each adjoining parish that was Acland land.

But fascinating as this history was, as we listened to Sir Antony we were reminded that the Aclands are now best known for their public service, generosity, and philanthropy. And modesty. Here talking to us gently and entertainingly was as fine an example of this distinguished family as any in this long and eminent line. A highly decorated man who had represented our country at Washington, had become head of the Foreign Office, and had worked closely with several Prime Ministers, especially Sir Alec Douglas Home and Mrs Thatcher, with a fund of (unfortunately presently unprintable) stories about these and many another eminent politician, reminisced quietly and self-effacingly, stroking his dog.

When you were a child, what did you want to be when you grew up?

I don't think I ever wanted to be an engine driver. I was at moments interested in Medicine, quite a few of my family having been doctors, which has continued with my own daughter. As my time at university drew to a close, I thought I'd try the Foreign Office exam – it was not too expensive to enter, several of my friends were having a go, and you didn't have specifically to prepare for it. One of my friends ran a book on the outcome, giving the unflattering odds of 14 to one that I wouldn't make it. A ten shilling bet in his own name that he put in his book as a long shot produced £7 10s, which paid for a slap up dinner for two in Woodstock.

And what was your favourite book?

John Buchan's novels. I read and re-read them all. Perhaps Greenmantle *was my favourite, though I also much enjoyed* John Macnab, *with those country pursuits.*

Who's had the biggest influence on you?

My Grandmother, who really brought me up. My parents were in the Sudan for much of each year, so my brother and I lived with her, in Berkshire. After the war when I was fifteen, my father inherited a house in East Devon, and we used to come up to North Devon and Somerset for outings and picnics, to learn about the Acland properties, which is how I came to know and love it here. We saw more of our parents from then on, but the strongest influence on me in those formative years was my grandmother, whose family also owned a property on Exmoor, where she was brought up. She was a tall good-looking woman, with a strong sense of right and wrong. Incidentally, also a very good water colourist. Later on in my Foreign Office career, Sir Alec Douglas-Home taught me a lot and had great influence

What's your happiest memory?

I have two of the happiest memories. I have been lucky enough to be married to two very special and wonderful women, my first wife dying in 1984.

What's your favourite colour – and why?

Green. It's the natural colour of the countryside. Did you see the fresh green of the beech trees as you came here?

Is the glass half full, or half empty?

Unfortunately, probably half empty. You see, throughout my professional life in looking after Ministers, I've always had to make sure that things were right, which means studying carefully where things might go wrong, to anticipate objections and to see the downside. So you have to check and re-check, be cautious and careful, and consider the risks.

What makes you angry?

Waste. Waste of anything, but particularly waste of goods and commodities. We are too profligate with the world's resources. It makes me angry that some 10% of all that's bought in supermarkets is thrown away. Also on Exmoor there is too much waste of trees and the thinnings from cutting and laying hedges. The brushwood ought to be shredded for wood pellets, not burnt. And we should learn to repair things again. Misrepresentation and injustice make me angry.

Tell us about something you'd really rather forget

Politely but firmly, Sir Antony declined to answer.

Where would you best like to be right now?

Here. I am content to be where I am. Certainly, not abroad. I have many friends locally and enjoy living here.

What present would you like for your next birthday?

Win the Lottery! I would then be able to give money to my children and grand children – I've nine grandchildren of my own, and my wife has twelve.

Later, as we prepared to go out with the dog, Sir Antony corrected this.
I think on reflection I would choose 'continuing good health.'

What's your biggest regret?

The untimely death of my first wife from cancer. But I was very fortunate to re-marry very happily after three years.

What have you done that you are most proud of?

I suppose climbing the greasy pole to become head of the Foreign Office. I was also head of The Senior Promotions Board, so was able to recommend myself as ambassador to Washington. I had two very interesting years with Ronald Reagan, and three with George Bush (Senior).

Please tell us a joke

By this stage, we'd been hugely entertained with many an amusing anecdote, such as a description of an occasion when he was Secretary to Selwyn Lloyd. Knowing he was away, he decided to make quick use of the private lavatory serving the very grand office of the Minister. Automatically, but in the event foolishly and unnecessarily, he turned the key – only to find the lock jammed. There followed a hair raising episode of clambering out of a window, with the Head of Protocol aiding the aerial Sir Antony with a stick, who ended spread-eagled round an outside pillar. Fortunately, the policeman below in Downing Street failed to spot a man apparently climbing into the Foreign Secretary's room. After this escapade, although Sir Antony asked a locksmith to check the working of the recalcitrant lock, he forgot to double check it himself. So later when a distinguished visitor availed himself of the small room and the key was heard to turn in the lock, Sir Antony assumed the worst. The Minister commented with surprise at the sudden pallor of his Private Secretary. Happily, in due course the key turned again uneventfully.

But it shows how you always have to be careful, to check and check again, and to imagine the worst case scenario.

Certainly, Sir Antony had no difficulty recalling many a joke.

An Ambassador, who assumed everyone recognised him, arrived at a hotel and was asked who he was? Loftily he told them if they did not already know, they would find the name on his luggage. Next morning he was even more displeased when his checkout papers were addressed to Mr and Mrs Genuine Rawhide!

Before we left, we took a pleasant stroll in Sir Antony's lovely millennium garden created by his wife, chatting about IT, the winter's casualties and horse riding, which exemplified somehow his wide ranging interests and concerns.

May that second birthday present request be fulfilled, with Sir Antony maintained in robust good health for many a long year yet – so that the Exmoor Society, and indeed the wider community, may continue to benefit from his fund of warm humour, good sense, sound balance, consideration and decency. And not least that admirable example of personal modesty and service to others.

HIGH GROUND HIGH POTENTIAL

R Thomas

In periods of great change, such as we are going through at the moment, with very difficult economic times, with cuts in public spending and greater awareness of global climate change and with the need for food and energy security, many bodies will be looking into the future to protect their own particular interests. Two such bodies, Natural England and the Commission for Rural Communities, have set out in recent reports their vision for the future of the English uplands. Natural England in a report "Vital Uplands a 20:60 Vision" states that if the uplands are sustainably managed then they will be able to provide a range of public benefits and services as well as food production. These include not only inspirational landscapes and habitats for rare and important species but more recently recognised services such as carbon storage and climate regulation, flood management and water supply. It argues that land management will need to focus on soils and peat resources, sustainable grazing and burning of upland heaths, bogs and grasslands, more and better managed woodlands, utilisation of green energy and low carbon growth in businesses and transport. The hope is that by adapting the ways in which the uplands are managed, the economics of hill farming will improve and the livelihoods of hill farmers and communities will be more secure. This vision is more than laudable but of course success will depend on the detail of how a particular place with its customs and practices is managed. Understanding the land management system honed through generations of farming on Exmoor, with its particular geology and soils, Atlantic climate and south-westerly location interacting with the local culture and business networks is crucial. What works in one upland area will not necessarily apply to Exmoor. Of course this report is only part of the story.

The Commission for Rural Communities in a report aptly named "High Ground, High Potential" likewise emphasises the wealth of both natural and cultural assets provided by upland landscapes and the need to realise their potential to secure a more prosperous future for upland communities. Recognising the harsh realities faced by these communities, it covers a wider field dealing with issues such as the need to invest in more affordable housing and improve access to next generation broadband and mobile communications. Interestingly however much of the report relates to hill farming and it states that the current support is inadequate to sustain the assets. A new approach is required that balances the needs of the environment with maximising the economic potential of the land. Farmers should be rewarded for managing natural assets in harmony with developing businesses. The report endorses the findings of the Society's *Moorland at a Crossroads* report in 2005 where I wrote that policies do not always pull in the same direction. A narrow focus, for example, on one aspect such as SSSI condition can lead to negative impacts on other interests such as archaeology, and farming systems are becoming disconnected from the moorlands because of inflexible restrictions. The report states that with little joined up thinking many well-intentioned initiatives have unintended consequences for people, and integrated rural development is required if the uplands are to unlock their potential. Ironically as this timely report brings together evidence of the severe problems facing upland communities so the decision has been made to abolish the national quango that provides a more holistic rural voice.

At the same time as these two important reports a new National Park Circular by government gives a vision for 2030 and updates policy guidance:

- *Thriving working living landscapes, notable for natural beauty and heritage*

- *Sustainable development in action, where people live within environmental limits and the services ranging from clean water to sustainable food are in good condition and valued*

- *Wildlife flourishes and is linked to ecological networks*

- *Places for escape, adventure, enjoyment, inspiration and reflection. Source of national pride and identity, fundamental to prosperity and well-being.*

To my mind, this is a rather vague and perhaps anodyne vision applying to the whole countryside and not emphasising sufficiently the significance of the natural and cultural assets and special qualities of national parks that require special protection and management.

Finally, in his interesting and stimulating article National Parks 2050 in this Review, Adrian Philips provides a vision by putting forward six propositions that he argues will set a different future from the present. The big question is how do we apply these propositions to Exmoor, protecting its national assets, growing their potential and securing livelihoods and a high quality of life for local people?

Resilient Landscapes: The mosaic of landscapes found on Exmoor will be part of its charm and subtle beauty with moorland, woodland, farmland, steep coombes and coast intermingling and providing stunning scenery, panoramic views and reinforcing peoples' connections with nature, history and their tangible and intangible values. It is the farming community in particular that has retained the long historical practices of moorland management including use of cattle, sheep and ponies and swaling patterns. Most important in the resilience to forces of change of this relatively wild landscape will be the continued dependence on local people and their knowledge and stockmanship skills. Otherwise, the moorland will become dominated by scrub and thorn trees making access impossible and other wildlife lost. Climate change will lead to some modifications but changing management practices will be the underlying cause. Farming families will still play an important part in the culture of the moor with tradi-tional events such as farm open days, farmers markets, agricultural shows, whist drives and hunt balls well appreciated by other local people as well as visitors who are recon-nected through such events with the land and its management. Opportunities taken for more woodland in the Brendon Hills and buffering of ancient woodland sites in places like the Barle and Exe Valleys will increase the overall percentage of woodland from the present 12%. People's perceptions of and preferences for Exmoor's different landscapes will have helped to guide decisions about the balance between the wild land and the farmed landscape.

Space for Nature: Exmoor will have more wild places including greater biodiversity and the restoration of upland bogs and heathland, and a network of hedges leading from the moorland edges to the enclosed farmland and beyond the park boundary into places like the Yeo Valley. Herds of wild red deer, the iconic symbol of the park are still present and the Exmoor pony, one of the oldest in the British Isles, will graze the moors and, like the deer, attract many visitors. Mosses, lichens and liverworts, rare butterflies and birds will still cling on and adapt to climate change. There are likely to be very few opportunities for introducing lost species because of Exmoor's overall small size and the rich variety of different habitats it already contains. The restoration of blanket bog on different sites protects the deep peat and has enhanced biodiversity, retained carbon stored in the peat and encouraged water retention and delayed peak river flows. The salt marshes at Porlock Bay are likely to extend inland and Porlock Weir will be inundated by the sea if the projected sea level rises are realised. The success of Exmoor as a national park will depend not only on its wildlife and visitor numbers but on the special qualities it provides such as tranquillity, closeness to nature, spiritual refreshment and understanding of its traditional rural way of life.

People and Jobs: With a greater recognition of the value of Exmoor's assets there will be more evidence of the link between the land resource and livelihoods and wealth creation. This is beginning to occur now for example by adding value to the primary products. As I wrote in the 2008 Exmoor Review, jobs and prosperity can be increased within the national park. The use of the Sustainable Development Fund in providing seed corn money to small businesses has encouraged many different ones such as a home delivery service of local products from local producers, a bracken composting company, a business selling seasoned netted logs and kindling and sheep identification, collection and genetic knowledge research leading to an easy care sheep. Heritage tourism will be a growth area with festivals and events offering a range of activities from walking, cycling and riding, discovering local heritage to those promoting local food, the arts as well as a variety of community ones such as Exford Horse Show and Hawkridge Revels. Micro renewable energy from different sources has been well developed.

Public Funds for Public Services Rendered: The increasing awareness of Exmoor's assets and the vital need to retain them in good condition emphasises the need for public money to be invested in the area. The recent announcement of public cuts however has led to the ENPA reducing its 2010/11 budget by £200,000 and facing further reductions in the next four years, leading to a likely £1 million loss in its grant aid support. Similar reductions in support are likely to affect other public bodies such as Natural England, and with the announcement of the abolition of South West Regional Development Agency there is concern over the loss of their investment in Exmoor and where the responsibility for CAP's rural development programme will lie. A strong case can be made for ENPA being delegated responsibility for agri environmental and rural development schemes and becoming more focused on land resources and unlocking potential income from the brand 'Exmoor'. By 2050 it is likely that the private and voluntary sectors will be providing more services that are outsourced by public bodies and stimulating entrepreneurial activity in conservation management.

Governance: It is difficult to envisage the likely governance of Exmoor in 2050 and whether the ENPA will be more of an enabler and less of an administrator or authority and based on the model of a Trust rather than working within local government. Certainly, the ENPA will be slimmed down with reduced membership and more rooted in the local community with direct elections. Planning and particularly development control functions may be delegated to local authorities working within the framework of the national park management plan. Membership of ENPA will include people with expertise in national park purposes and representing different interests but with the overall balance retained by local people.

New National Parks: National park status matters to Exmoor for it signifies that the area has a remarkable assemblage of natural and cultural assets that need protecting, managing and developing their potential to provide livelihoods, wealth, well being and services for society generally. There is always the danger of devaluing the currency by creating too many national parks, but there is an argument for creating one or two more with different kinds of landscapes and in locations nearer to large populations. Exmoor is very small and isolated compared with other national parks and the ENPA's focus and expertise on a farmed landscape and the enjoyment of it means that it could offer its services to other nationally important areas found locally. North Devon AONB, the Quantocks and Braunton Burrows Biosphere Reserve and the Lundy Marine Reserve could all be managed from Exmoor House as part of the greater Exmoor hinterland. This would leave the local authorities responsible for all their functions but helped by the Greater Exmoor national park in realising the full conservation potential and achieving World Heritage status as a cultural landscape of outstanding universal value. A future dream perhaps but then this is what visions are all about - aspiring for the high ground and unlocking the high potential.

THE NATIONAL PARKS IN 2050

A Phillips

What does the future hold for the National Parks? Using six propositions, this article looks forward to 2050. I make no claim to foresight, but the one thing we can be certain of is that the future will be very different from the present. It is an optimistic vision, but a challenging one. Rachel Thomas' response to these propositions, taking an Exmoor perspective, can be read in the previous article in this Review.

PROPOSITION 1: *National parks landscapes will become more resilient.*

By 2050, we will see a new landscape emerging in many parts of upland Britain, including our national parks. This will be more resilient to the forces of change, adapted to the fast changing climate, capable of storing carbon and water, and sustaining productive soils and wildlife. National parks will be places where we encourage pioneer economies and landscapes that can cope with accelerating change – though still respecting, and reflecting, the special qualities of these places.

That means a quarter of the parks will be forested, with mainly broadleaved woods and forests, double what there is now, because of the landscape, biodiversity, carbon, soil and water benefits of more treed uplands. The built landscape will change too: all *new* buildings since 2016 will have to be carbon neutral; all *existing* ones will be far better insulated. Solar panels, ground source heating, bio-mass boilers, bio-gas production and mini-wind turbines will be found on, in or under, nearly every building, and on every farm, in the national parks. Peak oil will triple the costs of fuel and fertilisers, and food policy will be driven by the quest for national and local self sufficiency. This will affect the landscape, for example in the added space given to growing vegetables, on farmland, in public parks and private gardens.

PROPOSITION 2: *More space will be made for nature.*

In this more treed landscape, there will be more opportunities for nature. Wilder places will be created in our national parks and some lost species (e.g. lynx, beaver, ospreys, cranes) will be reintroduced (or establish themselves). The tourist benefits of such initiatives will mean that parks will compete to be included in such schemes. National parks will be valued as much as havens for wildlife as for their beautiful landscapes; and the success of parks will be measured as much by their ability to attract wildlife as visitor numbers. Among novel schemes that will become commonplace are "eco-bridges" to enable wildlife corridors to cross roads and railways; coastal wetlands to absorb rising sea levels; and riverside washlands to accommodate flooding. A new generation of national parks (see below) will bring new habitats into the park family, such as flooded coastal wetlands and dry grasslands.

PROPOSITION 3: *The 'people and jobs' debate will look very different.*

Britain's national parks will still be protected, but lived-in, working landscapes. Already we have already moved beyond the "jobs v. beauty" arguments of the past, and now accept that beautiful parks support jobs, mainly in tourism but also because a good environment attracts and holds other kinds of business. By 2050, we will find that employment in the post peak oil economy is creating a new kind of beauty in the parks. The increasingly forested upland parks will pay their way, and create jobs, by providing essential services for society as whole – carbon capture and storage, water supply and regulation, timber and wood based industries, wildlife viewing, healthy living, adventure tourism, education and the like. At the same time, a vigorous small farming sector will thrive, with younger farmers, producing traditional high value foods mainly for local consumption and for visitors.

Together with this new farm economy will come many flourishing micro-businesses: food processing, craft manufacture, green energy innovation. The result will be a buoyant park economy, based on low impact activities, serving the local community and rooted in the physical qualities of the environment. The peak oil crisis that faces us in the next ten years will lead to radically different patterns of transport and tourism. The costs of motoring and the limitations of hydrogen and electric vehicles will make traffic jams in the countryside a thing of the past. Instead there will be a new interest in buses and rural light railways, serving local needs and bringing visitors to the parks by public transport in numbers not seen for a hundred years. Vistors will stay longer, make more use of local facilities and get to know the parks better; and thus the local economy will thrive.

PROPOSITION 4: *The parks will be paid for services rendered.*

The parks in 2050 will still be largely publicly funded but proportionately much more of the finance will come from sources other than the environment department. This is because the parks will have established that they play a vital role in promoting public health, crime prevention and education. They will be able to demonstrate that money spent on making the parks accessible for the public to use and enjoy is actually a better use of health, crime and education budgets than spending it remedially on hospitals, doctors, prisons and schools.

PROPOSITION 5: *The governance of the parks will change.*

By 2050, all park authorities boards will have adopted some variant of the "one-third/one-third/one-third" model:
- One third of members will be directly elected by local residents.
- One third of members will be appointed by a consortium of regional economic, environmental and social interests, including some places are reserved for elected local authority members.
- The final third will represent the national interest, but they will not be appointed by Ministers but in direct elections on-line by concerned members of the general public. Such "Friends of the National Parks" will have to meet certain criteria, e.g. frequency of visits to the parks or active membership of park-supporting NGOs.

PROPOSITION 6: *There will be new national parks*

A new generation of national parks will come into being in response to the changes in the climate, the need to adapt to these, the effects of peak oil, and the growing evidence that parks are good for the local economy. Possibilities include: a park focused on the National Forest of the English Midlands; a national park based on part of the Metropolitan Green Belt (the Abercrombie National Park?) and another in the Welsh valleys, both serving urban populations whose mobility will be reduced through peak oil; a Somerset Wetlands Park created after repeated tidal incursions have made conventional farming uneconomic; a Salisbury Plain National Park, based on former Ministry of Defence land and creating the largest dry grassland area in Western Europe; and several new parks in Scotland.

THE WORLD WAR II EXMOOR ROCKET

R McLaughlin

> *On Brendon Common, high up on Exmoor, at just about the summit of the desolate Lorna Doone country, there stands on end, on a two-foot square concrete plinth, a modest slab of rough-hewn granite: it marks the point where Bob Maclaren died.*[1]

There was not much tranquillity on Brendon Common seventy years ago. An inscription on the memorial gives us a hint: 'In memory of Colonel R H Maclaren OBE MC, Commander CW Troops, Royal Engineers, who was killed on duty on this spot May 20th 1941. This stone was erected by his brother officers.' How did the Colonel meet his death, on duty, in this bleak spot 1400 feet above sea level? What happened?

The business of the CW Troops was chemical or gas warfare. Colonel Maclaren's task was to develop a rocket delivery system for gas warheads. The legacy weapon from World War I was the Livens projector, a gas-filled drum fired from a steel tube buried in the ground. It was a static weapon, unsuited to a war of manoeuvre. In World War II, the British policy on gas was 'no first use'; but to be able to retaliate effectively, Britain needed a new gas weapon.

The new device was the five-inch rocket, comprising two cylindrical parts. One cylinder was the cordite-fuelled motor. The second, upper cylinder was the 30-pound gas warhead, developed at Porton Down. In gas trials there, targets included not only wild goats, but young soldiers too. Sapper Frederick Wright recalls lying on the ground near a scientific observer who, equipped with a gas mask (unlike Wright), recorded the effects of an aerial drop of poison gas on the unfortunate target. Happily, Sapper Wright survived, was posted to Exmoor, and is now alive, well and living in Suffolk.

Brendon Common was the location chosen for developing the rocket motor and a

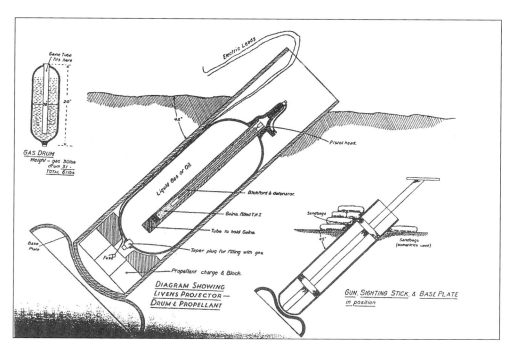

GAS DRUM
Weight – gas 30lbs
drum 31 .
TOTAL 61lbs

DIAGRAM SHOWING
LIVENS PROJECTOR—
DRUM & PROPELLANT

GUN, SIGHTING STICK, & BASE PLATE
in position

launching system, the responsibility of Colonel Bobby Maclaren. The lorry-mounted launcher, known as a 'sextuple', consisted of six troughs, each trough holding one rocket.

There were early problems: rocket casings were bursting when fired, and the weapon was nearly abandoned altogether. Eric Wakeling, a Sapper officer assigned to the rocket trials, volunteered for bomb disposal - thinking it would be safer.

There were numerous large-scale firings of the rocket on Brendon Common, sometimes at night - unlikely to go unnoticed by the local population. Mounted on ponies, John Pile with his father and Jack Edwards were tasked to clear the rocket range before a firing. They did not always succeed: as a 15-year old on the moor, Henry Richards remembers a rocket landing uncomfortably close. Some older inhabitants are still reticent about it now, constrained by the wartime duty of secrecy. One resident nursed a soldier suffering from toxic exposure, but doesn't like to speak about it – even today. There was at least one marriage between the soldiers and the local community: Sapper Stanley Wilde met his future wife Marjorie in Lynton when her parents' bathroom was commandeered for the soldier's use. Even at the end of his life, Sapper Wilde was reluctant to talk of his wartime duties on Exmoor, explicitly mindful of the Official Secrets Act.

What is known of the events of 20 May 1941? By then, the sextuple launcher was deemed ready for a demonstration to the decision-makers from the War Office. Returning to Brigadier Lloyd's account:

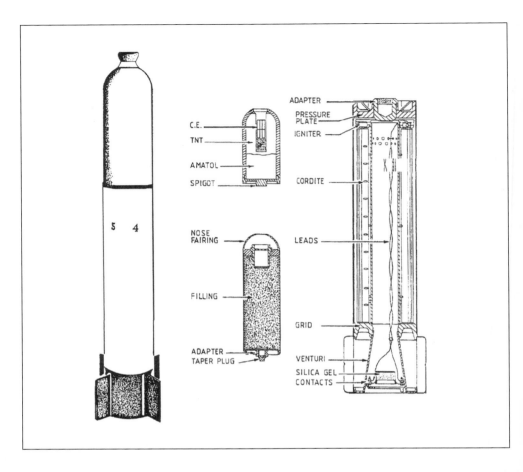

'Colonel Maclaren gave the order, and away went the first rocket. I was mystified when the second rocket flew higher than the first, and horrified when the third flew higher still. Soon a rocket went nearly vertically, and the next one past the vertical. I watched out for the rocket that had gone to the rear, and was relieved to see it burst harmlessly. The onlookers had stood their ground, and for a moment I thought we had got away with it. But then I saw that Colonel Maclaren was down.

'As was to come to light soon enough, a sliver of metal had flown at him, and had penetrated deeply in that utterly fatal area below the fifth rib. He was on his back, unconscious ... We tried to keep him warm with coats. Within half an hour the Medical Officer arrived with an ambulance; but it was too late. There was only the minor consolation that Bobby Maclaren had remained completely unconscious throughout.'

Above: *Rocket ship with rockets ready to fire*

Right: *Rocket ship firing rockets*

This tragedy, with concerns about reliability, might have spelt the end of the five-inch rocket. By 1942, gas could be delivered more effectively from the air, so the British Army abandoned the rocket; the Royal Engineers' gas warfare companies were disbanded, to the relief of all concerned. Whilst the rocket was never used for its original purpose – never fired in anger with a poison gas warhead – it had a spectacular reincarnation.

Here our story turns to Combined Operations. The calamitous Dieppe raid in 1942 suffered dreadful casualties, demonstrating that shore defences needed to be deluged with high explosive immediately before the assault troops landed. An accurate beach-barrage weapon was required. Thus was born the rocket ship: a landing craft converted to carry a thousand five-inch rockets, initially mounted in the Royal Engineers' sextuples.

The first operational use of rocket ships was in the Sicily landings in 1943. Each ship delivered half a ton of high explosive per second – for over a minute. 'When a rocket craft goes into action,' wrote Lt-Cdr Blackman RNVR, 'all the ship's company, with the exception of the CO who controls the firing mechanism from the bridge, go below decks. As the salvos are fired, there is a deafening roar like that of an express train, and a blinding sheet of red flame envelops the steel deck. Sometimes it is not possible to see the rockets reach their target because of the overhanging cloak of smoke and the choking cordite fumes. The decks would get red-hot from the back-fire but for the automatic water spray. After a succession of salvos, the decks are steaming with boiling water.'

On D-Day, thirty-six rocket ships were deployed, reducing Allied casualties significantly. The *Daily Telegraph* reported that 'rocket ships have been an immensely effective and terrifying weapon, discharging bank after bank of projectiles, and blasting the beaches with fire and destruction, until it seemed that no living creature could survive.'

One landing craft commander, Lieutenant Stuart Port RNVR (who later lived at Deercombe, near Brendon) wrote: 'When going into the beach, it was a little nerve-wracking to have a few thousand rockets sailing over our heads, and we always fervently hoped they had got the range right. At Walcheren, where they did not, fortunately I was to one side, heading for the gap blown in the dyke.'

In the October 1944 attack on the island of Walcheren, key to opening up the port of Antwerp, some rockets were misdirected at Allied landing craft - due to range-finding errors. The effect of the loose rockets, combined with incoming German artillery fire, can be felt in the laconic account of Lieutenant Cheney DSC RNVR:

'It was a horrifying experience as we disappeared under a black pall. The noise and blasting effects of the rockets made us feel as though we were being driven into the ground like tent-pegs. It was impossible to stand on the bridge, so I shouted into the voice pipe "Full speed – starboard 30" and we all threw ourselves on to the deck, hoping that we would swing out of the dreadful line of fire. Rockets were bursting on the deck and shell splinters were coming at us from all angles. Several Marines were injured when one rocket landed on the catwalk and another landed on the shield of 'B' gun. The barrage seemed to persist for an eternity before we swung away from the line of fire, and dealt with the wounded. The dreadful intensity of the sustained barrage, combined with the shelling from the shore batteries, did nothing to improve our morale. The gun-crews however quickly rallied, and we engaged the enemy battery again.'

The Americans devised a continuously-loading launcher for the rocket. The television (and DVD) series 'The World at War' showed this weapon in a short but awesome film sequence of the 1945 Okinawa landings. Bob Maclaren would have been proud, especially as his wartime obituarists were so constrained by secrecy. In the carefully circumscribed words of one, 'The value of his work will one day be recognised beyond the circle of those who were associated with him.' Hopefully, this article will widen that recognition. It is fitting to end with a tribute from a brother officer, Major General Tony Younger DSO OBE:

'Bob Maclaren was about the finest commander I ever served under.'

[1] Brigadier T I Lloyd CBE DSO MC, *Let's remember Bobby Maclaren*, Royal Engineers Journal, Vol. 95, No.1, 1981.

✧ ✧ ✧

THROUGH THE EYES OF A STAG – MY LIFE

J de Wynter-Smith

MUM'S STORY

I was walking through the tall reeds away from the herd of hinds I was with, descending into the valley of Tangs Bottom. It was early morning, with frost spread across the surface of the green grass. When I eventually reached the bottom of the valley a rabbit came squirming out of a bush which was full of crystal cobwebs. Then, the last thing I was expecting, a fox ran out after it.

When I finally got to the peaceful tree by the river where I wanted to give birth, I felt a splash by my hind leg, which was my bag breaking. I knew from that moment I was going to give birth that night. Soon the pains were getting worse and worse. Then I started to push as hard as I could push. The head finally came out so I could rest for a bit, but not long. I had my break and started pushing again. It was quite easy after I got the head out but it was still hard. I quickly jumped up, which was very painful. I turned around and started licking the warm afterbirth off. I noticed it was a little stag, which I was extremely pleased about.

MY YOUNGER LIFE

I was cold and wet and my mother was licking me all over. I was trying to get to my feet but I just didn't know how to walk. Five days later I could barely walk but I could walk just enough to move to somewhere safe where my mum could leave me. We set off on a journey up to the land of Exe-plain, the summit of the moor. It was wet, cold and windy up there but it would be warm in the reeds. At least I hoped it would be. When we arrived I was in my own little world whilst Mum was strutting around looking for a good place to leave me. I caught Mum's eye and I knew she wanted me to come over there and lie down. I lay down and I saw Mum walk off, leaving me for a day or two. Later on that day I heard footsteps coming closer and closer. Not my mum's footsteps, more like those two-legged creatures you see walking around the moor endlessly. I didn't know whether these creatures were kind or not. My heartbeat had gone right up and face was going very hot. As they got closer I heard them communicate in a strange language.

"What a lovely day it is Patrick. I wonder whether we will see any wildlife".

"Hey look there's something in the reeds, it looks like a baby deer".

That's when I really got scared.

"Ah, look at it, it's so cute".

"I told you we would see some wildlife on our walk".

They started to walk off into the horizon. I sighed in relief. I thought to myself I'd better get a good night's sleep ready for tomorrow. The next morning I was woken up by a horn which sounded extremely scary. The next minute my Mum came running up to me, head butting me gently to try and get me off the ground. I heard the horn again, then I heard dogs barking. My Mum started running so I attempted to keep up with her. My legs were aching like mad but I knew I had to keep going. As we were running my Dad and the rest of the hinds came running after us. My Dad was trying to keep us going. Dad pulled back to the back of the herd and kept running after us but then we heard a shot. We had to keep running but when we got to the horizon we stopped and looked around. It was my father.

MY MID LIFE

I had parted with my mother and I was living with a group of six bachelor stags. All we were doing was relaxing and building up our bodies so we were big enough and strong enough to challenge a stag in charge of a herd of hinds. The next evening it was cold, wet and windy, the grass was covered with frost. I was at the front of the group of stags heading towards a large field full of turnips. We were in a land full of risk but all of us thought it was worth it. Across the road from the field there was a half built house, which was why we didn't come in the day, because those weird two-legged creatures were working there. We knew it was mostly safe at night. When we were crunching the large turnips, a large two-legged and a small one started walking down the field. I was the first stag to see them. They started running and shouting. We started to run away and out of the field. We all jumped as high as we could over the tall fence and bank. When we were out, we kept running down into the moorland covered valley, which was filled with the sound of the River Barle trickling and meandering down the valley. We were safe down there.

The next morning it was like a flashback. I was woken up by the horn, this time I knew it meant death. All of us knew that. All of us quickly sprang to our feet and started running down the riverside. Then we noticed a group of horses running after us at the summit of the valley. Next I heard a shot and another. I looked around and saw one of my friends dead. I knew I had to keep on running. Over the weeks, I had nearly lost all my friends. I and the youngest one of the group were left. We were both struggling, but we knew that sometime, it would be our time to be the best.

FIVE MONTHS LATER

I was ready to challenge the best of the best. That night I started walking up the valley, heading towards the herd of hinds, which live by the bungalow at Titchcombe. It was a wet, cold and foggy night but found it quite easy to get there, because the stag was roaring and I knew where to go. When I got to the large field, I saw my rival and started walking right up to him. He saw me and I think he knew who I was straight away from past experiences we have had. He started running towards me, so I started running at him. When the antlers cracked together, the sound went straight through me. I couldn't quite get the energy to push him back but I tried. It was as if we were in a deadlock. I was starting to win. I was thinking "arr come on, you have to give up soon". Then he suddenly pulled away and ran across the fields. I knew I was the best of the best.

ONE MONTH LATER

I was now in charge of seventy hinds. I had led them back to my home. When we arrived I separated from my herd and walked down the valley through the tall reeds. I walked up to the peaceful tree where I was born and stood there, thinking. BANG! The shot echoed around the valley. I have had a brilliant life but I knew from the pain that hit me it was finally time to leave this wonderful place on Exmoor.

FIVE YEARS LATER

My sons became the best of the best, as I once was.

Lyn & Exmoor Museum – The Exmoor Society Connection

R Ferrar

This year finds our museum between two milestones. Last year we were thrilled to be awarded Full Accreditation by the MLA (Museums, Libraries and Archives Council), and then in 2012 we celebrate our 50th anniversary.

The museum is housed in St Vincent's cottage, a Grade 2 listed building tucked away in the Old Village area of Lynton. It was an ordinary, rather humble dwelling for centuries until acquired by Lynton Council in 1961. It was in poor condition, and proved difficult to let (possibly because it was haunted?) so was scheduled for demolition. A local resident, Harry Sutton, was fiercely opposed to this, and suggested it should be turned into a museum. With dogged perseverance he persuaded the council to let the cottage for a peppercorn rent. He was at that time secretary to the Exmoor Society, so it seemed reasonable that the lease should be signed over to them as trustees, but with a local committee to run and manage the museum.

The four trustees are named as John Coleman Cooke, Bob Nancekivell, John Pedder, and Harry Sutton. The Museum Management committee had 19 members, of whom only 2 survive; but they are still active: John Pedder is chairman, and Terry Loveless is treasurer. A bank account was opened with a donation of £40 from Billy Butlin, and £50 from the Exmoor Society.

A grand opening was planned for July 12th 1962; Lord Roborough to perform the ceremony, and a luncheon to follow at the Royal Castle Hotel. A list of "prominent people"

41

1962. Far left - John Pedder, then (as now) chairman of the Management Committee. Centre Lord Roborough. Far right may be John Coleman Cooke. The Mayor and Town Clerk are present as owners of the freehold.

was drawn up, but Lord Lytton returned his invitation giving his opinion that the cottage was too small, and it was "a ridiculous idea" to turn it into a museum. Most people were happy to accept, including Henry Williamson, author of *Tarka the Otter*. A proposal that Billy Butlin be invited was turned down.

The management committee was chaired then (as now) by John Pedder. Major Coleman Cooke (chairman of the Exmoor Society) was a founder member, but after 1964 his name does not appear in the minutes and it seems the management committee were left to run the museum autonomously. (However, Exmoor Society members are entitled to admission at concessionary rates to this day.)

In the 13 weeks the museum was open in 1962, 6,355 visitors had passed through the door. Six years later, the figure had accumulated to over 40,000. The historic stone-slab roof (thought to be the last remaining one in the National Park) had been restored at a cost of £625. A proposal that it be repaired with Welsh slates had (thankfully) come to nothing. In the 1970s, annual admission figures twice topped 10,000, but in 1999 the numbers were down to 2,100. Dr Mold (then chairman) wrote: "Our museum is in deep financial difficulty." From its inception the museum had employed a succession of dedicated "caretakers" - local pensioners who kept the museum clean, welcomed visitors and took their money. They could also be relied on to enliven a visit with their anecdotes of local life. (A favorite story was - and still is - of a ghostly presence in the back bedroom, linked to the discovery of concealed bones!) Initially they provided all this for a daily wage of around £5.

By 1999 door receipts were a mere £1,790, whilst the attendants' wages amounted to £1,300, leaving almost nothing to cover essential outgoings. Clearly, something had to be done. With trepidation the committee decided to dispense with paid staff and invited local residents to man the museum as volunteers. Fortunately, this worked and for the last 10 years, thanks to our willing helpers, the museum has continued its successful course. Sadly, our list of volunteers has become depleted, and we would gratefully

Mrs Sutton (Molly) and Ivy Williams, at the door of the museum, circa 1980. Ivy was the long serving attendant at the museum, always cheerful and full of local knowledge.

welcome any who could spare a 3 hour "slot" to man the door once a week, or less regularly. On a very wet day in 2002 the Duke of Edinburgh called to meet the committee and look around the museum. He clearly enjoyed his visit, as indeed do all our visitors judging by the enthusiastic comments in the visitors' book.

We are now putting together a funding bid to improve our facilities. Although we are keen not to lose the cheerful vernacular spirit which was Harry Sutton's hallmark, certain things need to be done. We need blinds for the windows and new dehumidifiers to control the micro-environment.

We hope to go over to LED lighting throughout. This has zero ultra-violet output and should also reduce our carbon footprint, as it uses one tenth the electricity of conventional lighting. We also plan audio-visual displays (not too intrusive!) and, in time, will digitise the whole of our photo archive and record all our exhibits on disc. We are quietly confident that visitors will continue to enjoy and learn from our museum for the next 50 years.

More information at: www.devonmuseums.net/lynton.

MOSAIC: BUILDING LINKS BETWEEN ETHNIC COMMUNITIES AND NATIONAL PARKS

C Taylor and D Rolls

Mosaic is a nation-wide project led by the Campaign for National Parks that works to engage young people and ethnic minority communities with the most spectacular and beautiful countryside in England – the National Parks.

Mosaic trains young people and leaders from ethnic minority communities to become volunteer "Community Champions" and promote the National Parks to others. This is achieved by giving Champions support, training and visits to the National Parks, as well as by helping them build relationships directly with National Park Authority staff and National Park Societies. The aim is for long term, independent contact.

Kathy Moore, CEO of the Campaign for National Parks, explains the need for Mosaic:

> "The National Parks were created sixty years ago for the benefit of the public. Only about one per cent of visitors to National Parks are from ethnic minority communities, although over ten per cent of the population is from an ethnic minority background. It is very important that a cross section of the British population develops a passion for National Parks and cares about their future protection."

Young people of all ethnicities face particular barriers in accessing wild areas such as National Parks, including lack access to transport, confidence and finance. Statistics from Exmoor National Park demonstrate the under-representation of young people:

Exmoor National Park Authority

- ENPA visitor surveys 2009/10: 2% of respondents were 16 to 24 years old

- ENPA volunteers 2009/10: 6% under 25 years old

- ENPA residents' survey 2010: 1.2% of respondents were 16 to 24 years old

Figures as provided by Exmoor National Park Authority

Defra's (The Department for Environment, Food and Rural Affairs) "Outdoors for All Diversity Action Plan" (www.naturalengland.org.uk/ourwork/enjoying/outdoors forall) provides a useful overview of the issues and specific barriers young people and ethnic minorities face in accessing the countryside.

So what does Mosaic mean for Exmoor National Park and the Exmoor Society? Key individuals from ethnic minority communities in Bristol, Exeter and Plymouth are being recruited to get involved with the National Park. And Mosaic Young Champions aged 16 to 25 years of all ethnicities, facing additional barriers such as disability, unemployment and low income, have been recruited from Plymouth, Exeter, Bideford and Barnstaple. They are all active in promoting Exmoor National Park to their peers.

The Champions' promotional role is supported by both the Mosaic team and the Exmoor National Park Education team, to ensure that Champions understand the fragility and vulnerability of Exmoor and want to protect it for future generations to appreciate and enjoy.

Together we are creating a new generation of people who respect and understand the special qualities of National Parks, and the need to protect their wild and varied landscapes.

The Mosaic model has proved to be a great success for both ethnic minorities and young people. A current Mosaic Community Champion explains:

> "Mosaic gave me the skills and confidence to help my community access the National Park. Before we would not have been aware of what was available there in terms of facilities, let alone the sheer natural beauty and that it was a place for us all to enjoy."

Mosaic has confirmed that there is a huge interest among ethnic minority communities to get involved with the National Parks. When the project started its operations in the north of England, it had a goal of recruiting 80 Champions but ended up with 200!

As the Minister for the National Parks, Huw Irranca-Davies MP, said at the Mosaic launch in July 2009:

> "Active engagement like this with contemporary urban Britain should be held up as a fantastic example to others on how to create long term change within many under-represented communities."

The Mosaic Young Champions were recruited in the summer of 2009 through a series of tasters events, including mountain biking and conservation. Autumn 2009 saw the young people staying at Minehead YHA for a "Champion Weekend". This residential enabled the young people to have a greater understanding of Exmoor's unique qualities and to plan their own projects that would enable their friends and peers to access Exmoor National Park.

Since then, the Young Champions have delivered their projects, which have ranged from world record attempts at tree planting to murder mystery tours. Young people are exploring in their own unique way how to make these treasured landscapes relevant and important to their generation.

For many of the 'Young Champions' the introduction to these special landscapes has resulted in a radical attitude change. One champion, Steve, says "the illusion has been broken that [it's] all about rambling. I've discovered that there's archery, gorge scrambling and high ropes – all kinds of fun."

The Young people are brilliant leaders and they make things happen. This is certainly true of Mosaic and the facts speak for themselves. In the last 6 months:

- 200+ days have been volunteered by the Young Champions
- 76 awards have been achieved by the Young Champions, for example the John Muir Award
- 100+ new young people have visited and tasted the unique qualities of the National Parks
- 1,000 hours have been spent in the National Parks by those young people
- 20 events have been developed by the young people
- 6 National Park services have been 'youth proofed'
- 100% of the young people have developed new skills and confidence

The Champions are benefiting in many different ways. Katie explains: "Through Mosaic, I've found new volunteers for my conservation project, I've made connections with the YHA and I have had help applying for funding." Steve adds, "I've met so many people and because I want to be a youth worker this project has helped me to develop the leadership skills I need." Khalil has learned to read a map and now believes he "can go anywhere." This is a ringing endorsement for Mosaic, which also aims to build life skills and leadership qualities in an outdoors environment.

In parallel to recruiting and training Community Champions, the Mosaic team and Exmoor National Park Authority staff are working together to develop and promote organisational change. Community Champions are helping the National Park Authority open its doors more widely to young and diverse communities, by advising on changes and contributing to decision-making.

For example, Caz, George and Sarah from a youth organisation called Switch in Bideford have been helping to "youth proof" the Exmoor National Park Authority's visitor services to help make their materials more appealing to younger audiences. This has resulted in the National Park Authority asking them to design a pocket guide about Exmoor targeting young people.

John Dyke, Chairman of Exmoor National Park Authority, endorsed Mosaic and highlighted how "the commitment and enthusiasm shown by the participants in the Mosaic project has been fantastic. The inspirational landscapes that are the National Parks will be safe in their hands especially as the Champions begin to influence and shape the work of the National Park Authorities as demonstrated through this project."

Looking ahead, the Mosaic work with ethnic minority communities is funded until 2012 so there is still plenty of time for the Exmoor Society to get more involved with the Exmoor Champions. And the youth project, which originally only had funding for 12 months, has recently been awarded additional funding from the Young Foundation through the Youth of Today programme, to extend the youth project in the south west. Key to this will be linking youth groups within the National Park with those on the periphery, such as Bideford, and wider afield, for example Bristol.

And finally perhaps we should leave the last word to CNP's President Ben Fogle. When recently interviewed about Mosaic he said, "It's not a good idea, it's a brilliant idea. For many Champions, Mosaic has given them a sense of belonging. I feel humbled and proud to have met them."

Well done to the Mosaic Champions; well done Exmoor National Park!

The Mosaic team is very keen to help our Champions get more directly involved with the Exmoor Society. If you would like to find out more about Mosaic's work with ethnic minority communities in Exmoor, would like to join in with a visit by Community Champions, or know of others who might be interested in becoming a Community Champion, please get in touch with Clare Taylor on: clare@cnp.org.uk or 07805 323 713. If you would like to find out more about the Mosaic Young Champions, please get in touch with David Rolls on david@cnp.org.uk or 07935 099 462. If you want more background about Mosaic in the National Parks, please visit www.mosaicnationalparks.org.

HAZEL EARDLEY-WILMOTT: A SEARCH FOR ORIGINS

F Presley

Ifirst became interested in Hazel Eardley-Wilmot when I came across *Ancient Exmoor* in Minehead public library. I was intrigued by her description of the Neolithic stones on Exmoor, especially the unique 'stone settings' in their extraordinary geometric patterns. However, as I continued my research, I realised that, as a writer myself, I was drawn as much by the quality of her writing as by the subject of her research. There are other books on the archaeology of Exmoor, and some more professional and scientific, but none were as well written as hers in terms of literary style, as well as reference to literature, etymology, and the classics. In the short preface to the book she describes herself as an Oxford graduate in English, a serious amateur archaeologist, with a variety of experience in other professions, both in England and abroad, and 'some acquaintance with the vagaries of language'. She had, she tells us, spent nearly fifty years gradually becoming familiar with the moor.

In a collaborative writing project with the poet Tilla Brading, I have explored Neolithic sites and spoken to archaeologists, some of whom remembered Hazel Eardley-Wilmot, and a larger than life character began to emerge. There were even rumours that she had been a spy during WW2! We learnt that she would boldly go out waving her stick while you followed in her wake – this was the famous walking stick with a six inch nail used to prod for stones. It was two or three years after beginning our research that we made contact with Hugh Thomas, Eardley-Wilmot's friend and literary executor, and discovered what a wonderful archive exists of her papers and artefacts. Some of these are held at the Thomas' house, while the bulk of the papers she considered important are held by Oxford University, mainly at her old college of St Anne's.

Born in 1910, Eardley-Wilmot went to St Anne's in 1928. Last year I spent some time looking through the papers at St Anne's, and was very surprised to discover that there were three unpublished books, all dating from the late 1940s. I hadn't known how serious she was, when young, about becoming a novelist and historian, and how much she achieved in a burst of energy and writing, which all relates to her six years work with the Czechs for the British Council. The books consist of *The Broken Curve,* an historical memoir of post-war Prague before the Communist take over in 1948; a satirical novel, *Coffin's Burden,* which is about Britain's cultural ambassadors abroad; and *Thursday's Child or The Traveller,* an allegory of the state of Europe in the mid-twentieth century, and the heroine's (her) attempt to find a place within it. All three books represent a creative, dynamic phase in her life when she was at the centre of European politics and culture. *Thursday's Child* seems to have been the most ambitious of the three books, and the one that mattered most to her. It is a re-working of the *Odyssey,* which also made me think of *Pilgrim's Progress,* for its moral concerns, if not its theology, and of Albert Camus' great war time novel of the city, *La Peste.*

I get the impression that when she failed to get published, and had to earn her living, first as a teacher, then as an education officer, she lost faith in her future as a professional writer. I wonder whether she was also unsure how to situate herself in the post-war political landscape of this country. She had witnessed the ruthless battles of fascists and communists in Europe, and the extinguishing of freedom in Prague with the Communist coup d'état. She had become deeply involved in Czech politics and seen the terrible fate of Jan Masaryk. In her journal of 1947 she writes:

> Drained now by two days in which it has been impossible for me to think of feel anything but this – his own suffering, and this for Anna and for all Czechs and how it is for the whole human predicament. His longing for one human world – still trying for that, for some vestige of freedom for his own people, till five minutes past the hour – then no hope of either – the world irrevocably split.

Eardley-Wilmot was eventually to enter a new phase of creativity and reinvent herself as the author of books on Exmoor's history. One of the continuities, between the two most creative phases of her life, is her love of nature. I think it must have been shortly after leaving Oxford in 1931 that she spent some time as a governess in South America. She was a keen horse rider and enjoyed life on the pampas. She was also perhaps influenced by the writings of the naturalist W. H. Hudson, who grew up in South America, and whose work she admired. We know about the South American connection from a photo album in the Thomas' archive, and from articles she wrote under the pen name Anne Marow.

More significantly much of her writing in the late 1940s was done while she was staying on Exmoor. There is an attention to the natural world in *Thursday's Child*, and the heroine's childhood is spent in a rural landscape, near the source of the river, which is the central metaphor of the novel. She has an intimate knowledge of flora and fauna: 'She would look for the tiny grey-green trumpet of lichen, with its scarlet drum-knob of flower, a sentry motionless at his post on the boulder of live quartz.' However the heroine, Rosalind, like Eardley-Wilmot, is drawn to the city – first the City of Fair Learning (clearly meant to be Oxford) and then to the city of Duality, which is divided between the haves and the have-nots. Eardley-Wilmot lived both in Prague and London, but ultimately returned, as Rosalind does, to the country. She writes in her journal: '(Rosalind) should draw on this country continuity - piercing quietly through to it wherever she is…', and, 'trees – here – in Czia – this intense feeling of the <u>life</u> of each tree, stronger in winter than in summer – the sense of vitality in pause'. Like other pioneering women writers of the last century, such as Virginia Woolf and Dorothy Richardson, Eardley-Wilmot reaffirmed her sense of self through an intense and joyful affinity with the natural world.

Disillusioned by political ideology, there is also an absence in Eardley-Wilmot's work of religious doctrine, which may have been partly due to her education, and also, perhaps in reaction to her father, who was a vicar. Nor is she tempted, as many others were, to mysticism.

If this was mere human resilience, said the soul, was that so 'mere'? And to disparage this obstinate resurgence as animal ... what hubris was that? Rosalind could not feel so separate from animal or bird, flower or tree.

Later in this crucial chapter from *Thursday's Child* we find:

She sank to her knees and bowed. To what? She could not have said; but for the glimpse into a depth past sounding, in reverence simple and undivided, there was no other position possible.

This is the closest she can come to prayer, to a 'depth past sounding', which is 'merely' the depth of human, and natural, history.

Eardley-Wilmot retained her interest in humanity, and if she distanced herself from the crisis of twentieth century politics, she was still able to take a long view of society as an archaeologist. In her last book *Yesterday's Exmoor*, published in 1990, when she was 80, she also paid tribute to the community on Exmoor, where she finally made her home. Recently, with the help of Richard Westcott, we have interviewed friends and neighbours of Eardley-Wilmot in and around North Molton, who still have vivid and affectionate memories of her. Eardley-Wilmot may have abandoned fiction, but her interest in language, and the 'vagaries of language', grew stronger over time. She was a keen linguist and etymologist, compiling a dictionary of dialect words and exploring the significance of names, whether of places or Neolithic longstones.

Although Eardley-Wilmot is now known as a local historian of Exmoor, she deserves to be seen in a much wider context. We have only skimmed the surface of the archives, and there is a need for more research as well as reassessment and publication of some of her earlier work. This would give us a much more complete sense of a remarkable woman and writer.

THE WEST SOMERSET FREE PRESS

J Cox

When a Williton printer Samuel Cox first published the *West Somerset Free Press* in July 1860, Frederic Knight was finally making progress with his father's grand project to reclaim the ancient Royal Forest of Exmoor.

The main farms had been established, grazing land was being won and new strains of sheep were beginning to thrive. Knight was even considering building a railway, from Simonsbath to Porlock, hoping he could emulate the success of the Brendon iron mines to the east, and extract iron ore.

There is little mention of such developments in the first editions of the *Free Press*. But from the start, one activity on the moors is regularly reported: naturally, it was hunting.

On September 8th, 1860, the paper carries its first hunt report – a meet of the Devon & Somerset Staghounds at Whitestones on Porlock Hill, attended by "a large number of lovers of this noble sport."

But even this far back, controversy stalked hunting. The D & S Master, Mr Mordaunt Fenwick Bissett was moved to write to the *Free Press* in October 1867 after the *Daily Telegraph* had reported that a hunt from Selworthy had ended at Bossington with a deer "… left drowning, or lying maimed and bleeding at the bottom of a crag, after having been pursued with a broken leg over miles of country."

Mr Bisset was resolute in his defence:

"I have no intention of entering into any controversy as to the cruelty of stag-hunting.

"I am quite content to leave my character in regard to cruelty to animals in the hands of the public of whom, I am proud to say, a still increasing number come, year after year, to witness and patronise what you are pleased to term our 'sport royal'". October 12th 1867.

Perhaps, more surprisingly, as early as 1875, the *Free Press* was reporting the first signs of a moorland conservation movement; even then, some were concerned at the sight of ploughs cutting into the unspoilt turf of Exmoor.

'Bad news for lovers of picturesque scenery and grand views of heather-clad moorland. Mr Knight – the owner of the greater part of Exmoor – has, or will shortly have, one of the Duke of Sutherland's ploughs for breaking up rough ground and proposes, I hear, trying it on Exmoor.

'And to make bad worse, I understand that Sir Thomas Acland, almost if not quite as large a moorland owner as Mr Knight, has been to Scotland, and has come back, much struck by the Duke's improvements and thinks of going and doing likewise on Exmoor, and so spoiling some

of the prettiest scenery and wildest hunting in the South of England.' October 16th 1875.

Four years later, Exmoor and the D & S was honoured with the visit of the most distinguished of visitors - the Prince of Wales, later to become King Edward VIIth.

Prince 'Bertie' was well-known for his playboy lifestyle, having little constitutional role during the long life of his mother, and the *Free Press* reported at great length his stay with the Luttrells at Dunster, and his day's hunting at Hawkcombe Head.

At the end of a two-hour chase, the stag stood at bay at Badgworthy Water.

"The Prince cut its throat, the mort was sounded, and cheers long and loud were given.

'According to ancient and irrefragable custom, His Royal Highness was "blooded," Mr John Joyce respectfully performing this most ancient ceremony which consists of sprinkling some of the stag's blood on the novice's face.' August 23rd 1879.

Not long after this, the *Free Press* mourned the death of the Master of the D & S. The obituary reflected the general view that Mr Bissett's appointment as Master in 1855 was the saving of both of the red deer herd and of staghunting on Exmoor.

'At that time, the hunting of the red stag in its native wilds of Exmoor was only carried in a feeble and half-hearted manner and threatened to become extinct. With the advent of Mr Bissett, a new state of things was inaugurated. A taste for the good old sport was revived and after four years of varying fortunes, the pack of staghounds came under the able Mastership of Mr Bissett

who improved the hunt to a marvellous degree.' July 12 1884.

The paper reported the first stirrings of modern-day tourism on Exmoor with the arrival in the summer of 1914 of the first 'char-a-bancs'. These 17-seater open-topped motorised coaches offered 50-mile tours from Minehead to Lynmouth, Simonsbath, Exford and home via Cutcombe. They were not universally welcomed, competing for space on the narrow moorland roads with the last of the horse-drawn stage coaches and riders on horseback. But finally, Exmoor was being opened up to visitors.

Two events on Exmoor in 1931 transfixed not just readers of the *Free Press*, but the national papers as well. First, in April, the remains of a 16-year-old Exford girl – Mollie Phillips – were found in a bog on Codsend Moor. Her disappearance 18 months earlier and the subsequent searching of the moors had made national news.

An inquest held in Minehead returned a verdict of accidental death, but at the funeral, the Vicar of Cutcombe caused an outrage when he said the jury understood nothing about Exmoor and that everyone on the moor believed that Mollie had in fact been murdered.

Fleet Street's reporters flocked to the moors; the police staged secret excavations at night, cheque books were waved, but eventually, after a heartfelt appeal from Mollie's mother, the incident subsided.

But by August, the reporters were back again; the opening meet of the D & S at Cloutsham had attracted a mass protest mounted by the League for the Prohibition of Cruel Sports.

The *Free Press* reported that the protestors were confronted by massed ranks of hunt supporters. There was a dense fog, and actual hunting was out of the question.

'A woman it was – an Exmoor farmer's wife – who captured the first banner. Grabbing it from one of the ladies of the party - there was a bit of a tussle for possession – she tore it fiercely to tatters and amid the cheers of the crowd, trod the fragments into the road.

'Others strove to gain possession of banners and in the midst of an excited mass, the demonstrators struggled helplessly. Their banners were all destroyed, the women's umbrellas wrecked, the League literature ripped to fragments.' August 8th 1931.

While all this was going on, the newly-formed British Field Sports Association had set up in an outbuilding of Cloutsham Farm; 200 new members were enrolled.

Reporting of events during the Second World War were severely curtailed by the censor's pencil; there are no mentions of the massed Allied manoeuvres on the moors, of the American gunnery ranges on Larkbarrow and elsewhere, or of the enormous tented encampments on Winsford Hill and the Brendons.

And, of course, we would have to wait until after the war was long over to read an account of the visit to Dulverton of the Supreme Allied Commander General Dwight D Eisenhower, only weeks before the D-Day invasion.

But before the war was over, in 1944, the *Free Press* reported at length on the biggest single donation of land to the nation, when Sir Richard Acland gave to the National Trust his entire Holnicote Estate; 6,000 acres of moorland and 4,000 acres of arable land between Dunkery Beacon and North Hill that included the villages of Selworthy, Bossington, Allerford and Luccombe.

Public access to the moor was to be a driving issue for the rest of the twentieth century. In the early 1950s, the *Free Press* regularly reported the initial widespread opposition to the idea that Exmoor should be designated a National Park. "The happy ideas of a lot of idealists" said one member of Dulverton RDC, "fantasies of the urban mind."

Despite this, in 1954 the Exmoor National Park came into being – but the new park did not include the Quantock Hills, as had first been proposed. That, it was said, might come later.

For the next forty years or so, the *Free Press* reported on the inevitable battle between those concerned to protect the unspoilt landscape of the new National Park, and the farming community tasked to produce food for the nation and to make a living for themselves and their local workers.

The first battle was, in fact, over the Forestry Commission's plans to plant conifers on The Chains, a plan successfully opposed by a loose group of conservationists who later formed themselves into the Exmoor Society in 1958.

The tussle over how best to develop the moor and the moorland economy regularly made headlines in the *Free Press* in the 1970s; the conservationists thought the Porchester report in 1977 had answered their demands, with conservation orders and compensation payments, but the NFU opposed it and the proposals fell with the Labour government in 1979.

By the 1980s, locally-agreed arrangements took the heat out of the argument and attention soon turned to finding ways to boost the moorland economy.

Beast spotted chasing deer

THE beast of Exmoor killed at least two sheep in the Dulverton area at the weekend—but the latest eye-witness accounts suggest that it may now be turning its attention to deer.

Police now believe that the beast, which has claimed over 100 sheep along southern Exmoor, is a lurcher dog.

After the weekend killings, Avon and Somerset police held urgent talks on Monday with the Devon and Cornwall Constabulary to plan joint operations.

As a result, the marine sharp-

"It was a scruffy-looking thing about the size of an alsatian," said Mr. Floyd, "It reminded me of a lurcher.

"But it made a funny noise like a bear. I have never heard an ordinary dog do that. It was about 50 yards behind the deer."

Mr. Floyd was working on the Hollam Estate, near Barlynch Abbey. Directly opposite is the League Against Cruel Sports' Barlynch Woods sanctuary where hundreds of deer roam.

Despite the killings, Winsford Hill farmers are not yet organising themselves in the way that South Molton farmers did, with posses ready on the end of telephone lines.

While this was going on, the *Free Press* was, of course, reporting the other events on the moor; the appearance of The Beast of Exmoor in 1983; the thwarted attempts to build a 'golf-ball' radar dome on Shoulsbarrow; Paul McCartney's purchase of land on the moor as a deer sanctuary; and of course the growing political pressure on hunting.

Over the last decade, the *Free Press* has devoted hundreds of column inches to the Hunting Act's ban on hunting mammals with hounds, its impact on Exmoor and the ultimately failed prosecutions through the courts.

And for almost the whole of 2001, the issue of foot and mouth was never out of the headlines; the threat of the disease, and then its eventual arrival in the Wiveliscombe area effectively closed the moor, made farmers virtual captives on their own land and brought tourism to a shuddering halt.

Staghounds charges dropped

A LENGTHY three-year legal battle has finally come to an end for three members of the Devon and Somerset Staghounds who had been accused of breaching the controversial Hunting Act.

All charges have been dropped against joint master Maurice Scott, huntsman Donald Summersgill and whipper-in Peter Heard after the Crown Prosecution Service (CPS) decided not to pursue the case.

The decision ends a three-year nightmare for the men, whose arrest sparked outrage among members of the rural community when it was revealed Mr Scott had been arrested and locked up in a urine-soaked police cell.

The three were charged in 2006 follow-

ing as a whole," he said.

"We were always convinced that what we were doing was legal and, while we all hope that the Hunting Act does not last much longer, the Devon and Somerset Staghounds will be able to continue some form of hunting and deer management until it is repealed."

It is the second time in recent weeks that the CPS has backed down against a huntsman, having decided not to challenge a ruling that found in favour of Tony Wright of the Exmoor Foxhounds.

Mr Wright became the first huntsman to be prosecuted and convicted under the Act but subsequently had his conviction quashed.

He maintained he had simply been using two hounds to flush out foxes to be shot, something allowed within the terms of Act

In 2009, as the *Free Press* ended its first century and a half reporting events on Exmoor and the wider district, it was clear that the fiercely independent folk of the moors would continue to make headlines; concern over plans to demolish a lonely herdsman's cottage at Blackpitts, near Simonsbath, led to the formation of the Revolting Exmoor Peasants Party.

There were clearly going to be many more stories from Exmoor in the *Free Press*.

Read a book review on Jeff Cox's new title
West Somerset in the News *on page 107.*

A Silver Thread in the Landscape

T Oliver

Exmoor's relative remoteness has become one of its attractive characteristics. Nurturing the specialness of being a place which is harder to get to is now firmly part of planning a successful and prosperous future for Exmoor. Now, a short-lived and previously unsuccessful attempt to make the western part of Exmoor more accessible a century ago, could offer a fascinating combination of distinctiveness and accessibility which at the same time reduces the pressure from conventional road transport. This startling combination presents itself in the form of the re-awakening Lynton and Barnstaple Railway. To see just how this might happen, people living on Exmoor can look at a precedent in Snowdonia, where the **entire** rebuilding of the Welsh Highland Railway is reaching completion.

Previously remote from railways, Lynton and Lynmouth were connected with Barnstaple in 1898, by a narrow gauge line. It was built at the diminutive gauge of just under two feet. Small-scale lines had the supposed benefit of cheaper construction. But the marginal viability of such a limited size of railway operation was soon apparent as the age of the private car and lorry arrived within 20 years of the line opening. Despite popularity with summer tourists, the picturesque and charming Lynton and Barnstaple closed in 1935. The Welsh Highland Railway, even more of a tourist operation than the Lynton and Barnstaple, similarly succumbed a year later.

In the 1950s, the slate-extraction railways of Snowdonia were gradually revived, the first time in the world that railways had been taken over and run by volunteers for tourists. Known as the Great Little Trains of Wales, this group of formerly industrial railways which wind their way into the foothills of Snowdonia, now attract visitors from all over the world. These railways offer an extraordinarily effective way of bringing people through delicate and beautiful landscapes with minimum intrusion. The small-scale engineering, originally driven by economy, excels at threading its way through outstanding landscapes with great charm and offering breathtakingly intimate contact between passengers and their surroundings. These railways also bring with them a celebration of much outstanding cultural and built heritage, nurturing a remarkable range of traditional skills in construction and maintenance of our best Victorian engineering and design.

For more than sixty years, the Lynton and Barnstaple railway remained but a poignant element of north Devon's archaeology, its modest, often serpentine earthworks still conveying some of the line's character. Part of the line was converted into a public road during the deep snow of 1962-3, a small viaduct was blown up as a practical demonstration during the war and a short stretch of the line was drowned by the filling of Wistlandpound reservoir in the 1950s. But luckily, most of the alignment remained intact. Most remarkable of all, the palely graceful eight arches of Chelfham viaduct were kept properly maintained; the tallest narrow gauge railway structure in Britain.

In the early 1990s work began to re-open the Welsh Highland Railway. The idea was, from the outset, to provide a means of getting visitors into and through the national park following the dismantled trackbed abandoned since 1937, in both an unobtrusive and spectacular way. This combination of qualities, drama for passengers and discretion for those appreciating the outstanding landscape of the Aberglaslyn Pass, prevailed. The Secretary of State overturned an Inspector's recommendation for refusal at public inquiry in 1999 despite the initial opposition of the Snowdonia National Park Authority. Some of the route of the railway had become a public right of way and an important part of the revival of the line was to retain the route for walkers as well as the rebuilt railway.

The rebuilding of the Welsh Highland railway, from Caernafon to Porthmadog has cost over £14m and taken more than 13 years. The revival of this spectacular route celebrates the beauty of its surroundings and offers a subtle and effective way to allow many people to witness Snowdonian grandeur and landscape character. The railway has already had two royal visits.

The same could happen on Exmoor. The revived Lynton and Barnstaple railway is already in business, running from the highest station on the line, Woody Bay, towards Parracombe and offering a compelling mixture of exhilarating views towards Heddon's Mouth, an often wild and blustery journey across high pastures and arrival at a beautifully restored late 19th century railway station which acts as a distant lodge to the demi-alpine mood of Lynton and Lynmouth. Crucially, the revived railway is faithful to the great beauty of the surrounding Exmoor landscape.

Hugely to its credit, the National Park Authority has allowed the railway to become established. The North Devon Local Plan has an excellent policy, REC4, which anticipates the reconstruction of the railway back towards Barnstaple and protects the route. The Greater Exmoor Sustainable Economic Development Strategy similarly anticipates the contribution of a revived Lynton and Barnstaple railway in the service of the National Park, in Actions 20 and 21, improving public transport and making car free travel easier into the National Park.

By reducing car use, thereby helping Exmoor remain tranquil, allowing visitors to appreciate the changing landscape approaching and passing through Exmoor from the west and encouraging volunteering, a fully rebuilt Lynton and Barnstaple railway could play a central part in Keeping Exmoor Special. A rare and exceptional feat of unintrusive and charming infrastructure (and how much new infrastructure deserves that description?) could be revived to beckon visitors to Parracombe, Woody Bay, Lynton and Lynmouth by way of Blackmoor Gate and Wistlandpound. The railway would conjure visitors from their cars on the edge of the park or even in Barnstaple, and introduce them to the intimate delight of combes, moors and deep woods at a pace in harmony with appreciation of the character of Exmoor. Engineering which even in the 1920s and 1930s was seen as exceptionally in sympathy with its surroundings and which appealed immensely to the hearts of visitors and residents alike, could find a new and hard-working role as a silver thread leading to the heart of the ravishing beauty of Exmoor.

What is needed now is a concerted effort of imagination and commitment. Already, the revived railway has cost £1million. Expenditure on the same scale as the Welsh Highland's £14 million would see substantial progress towards a completed railway, bringing great economic as well as environmental and cultural benefits. The private sector needs to be encouraged to play its part, as Nuttalls, the engineering firm which originally built the railway already has, by building and donating a new bridge for the line. The prudent work of Exmoor Associates, buying land along the route as it becomes available, and managing this land sympathetically, is setting a fine example.

Snowdonia has demonstrated how to revive railways at a scale delicate enough to compliment the finest of landscapes. Exmoor and North Devon have already shown great foresight in their plans. In its award winning work on conserving the archaeology of the West Somerset Mineral Railway, the National Park Authority has shown that it understands the contribution of rural railways to landscape character and cultural inheritance. The Lynton and Barnstaple railway could be part of the Greater Exmoor Vision for tourism and recreation in 2017.

CANOEING ON EXMOOR: A PERSONAL VIEW

P Carey

You may have noticed an increasingly common sight when walking along fast flowing Exmoor rivers – canoeists skilfully negotiating terrifying rock-strewn rapids. Whilst the occasional canoeist may have been seen on some stretches in years past, the recent escalation in their number has been dramatic, prompted in part by an assertive and uncompromising stance taken by the canoeists' representative body 'Canoe England'. Individual reactions to this phenomenon vary between approval of a healthy outdoor pursuit; and annoyance at an unwelcome (and sometimes unauthorized) intrusion into an otherwise undisturbed natural landscape. On sober reflection several important questions arise.

Does the purchase of a canoe confer a right to float anywhere?
There is no general right of public navigation in non-tidal waters in England and Wales[i]. The river bed is owned, normally privately, though sometimes by a public body, but in either case permission is generally needed for canoeing, or other watersports, to take place. Without this permission, such activity amounts to trespass and, in relation to the owner of fishing rights, can constitute an actionable interference with existing rights[ii]. Navigation rights such as those on the Thames may be established by Act of Parliament, grant by the relevant owners, or through immemorial use of a particular waterway, but such circumstances are unusual. In practice this means that, on Exmoor, in order for

canoeing to take place lawfully, there needs to be a voluntary access agreement between owners and would-be users or some form of explicit permission for such use.

Riparian owner associations[iii] can help develop such agreements by representing the views of members. Riparian owners have in some cases legitimate concerns about privacy and unreasonable interference with the enjoyment of their own property. They also have certain important legal obligations in relation to the watercourse itself and typically a strong interest in its well-being. Arguably too, in this crowded island, owners have a moral obligation to try to facilitate responsible access.

Unfortunately, progress is currently impeded by Canoe England's insistence on year round canoeing[iv] and the rejection of the right of any riparian owner to restrict the where and when of access. The canoeists' representative body is, of course, entitled to lobby government for free legal access[v] to all inland waters, although it is difficult to see why canoeists should be given priority over the array of other activities now possible on or in water. But it is unrealistic, as matters stand, for it to seek to dictate access terms. Canoe England's stance has encouraged the mistaken, but self-serving, belief amongst a significant body of canoeists that they are entitled to paddle anywhere at will. It has also made the negotiation of further agreements by its own local officers much more difficult.

Are unregulated watersports acceptable within the National Park?

Traditional country pursuits have latterly been joined on Exmoor by several extreme sports. However, its rivers and streams have, until recently, remained relatively untouched by newer forms of activity and provide important natural reserves and highways for wildlife. It is clear that canoeists now travel considerable distances to experience the Exmoor rivers, the commercial exploitation of which for watersports appears increasingly likely. Does this matter or are canoeists simply a welcome addition to the overall visitor numbers?

National Parks are special places, with tranquillity one of their valued qualities. The importance of both 'conservation' and 'public access' was recognized from their inception, but in cases where these purposes are in conflict the well known 'Sandford Principle' establishes the priority of the former[vi]. The point at which the pressure for increased watersports access compromises a locality is a moot issue. In its policy on canoeing the Exmoor Society advises against any extension of existing canoe access agreements, unless it can clearly be shown that an appropriate balance is being struck between this activity and broader environmental and recreational interests. It may be that this balance will become more difficult to strike in the face of strident demands for increased sporting opportunities.

Is canoeing harmful?

In 2009 Natural England, following an appropriate assessment, consented to an application by the National Trust to permit winter-only canoeing on the East Lyn downstream of Watersmeet, subject to water level and for a trial three year period. The former has an important legal role in this case as the stretch forms part of a Site of

Special Scientific Interest and Special Area of Conservation. It would be unfortunate if this consent was seen as a 'green light' to canoe in conservation areas generally, as the assessment is predicated on canoeists complying with the terms and advice associated with the particular access arrangement.

Natural England's assessment of the Lyn provides an initial framework for the consideration of the ecological impact of canoeing more widely and helps to identify the current gaps in knowledge. The range of key riverine Exmoor species that must be considered includes salmonids - salmon eggs in the redds, which are formed in autumn and early winter, can easily be damaged or disturbed and washed out[vii]; mammals, especially the otter; nesting birds, notably kingfisher, grey wagtail and dipper - which may have eggs in the nest by late February; and the often overlooked bryophytes and lichens, some of which, such as the river jelly lichen, are extremely rare. Adverse effects might occur as a result of disturbance or abrasion, degradation of habitat (for example by removal of woody debris to facilitate passage) or by the introduction of disease, pests or parasites.

Does canoeing represent a substantial ecological risk? The best answer currently available appears to be that "it all depends". Key factors are the nature and size of the river, its native population, the intensity of canoeing - and the willingness of canoeists to acknowledge potential risks, respect sensible restrictions and adopt (together with other stakeholders) a precautionary approach to watersports in sensitive environments whether formally protected or not.

Should watersports access be managed?
Given the special nature and profile of the National Park, users' sometimes conflicting recreational interests, and the clear legal obligations[viii] towards the conservation areas within it, the answer to this question would appear self-evident. Surprisingly there has been very little active engagement with this developing issue by the authorities.

Canoe access has been cast by the Exmoor National Park Authority as essentially a matter between private individuals, i.e. the canoeists and the riparian owners, with little recognition of any public interest dimension. In its desire to promote access the Park Authority has positioned itself simply as a broker of canoe access arrangements. Sadly, this strategy for managing unauthorized, sometimes environmentally inappropriate, activity based more or less exclusively on the promotion of additional access is wholly inadequate.

The default position is that responsibility for 'managing' canoe access on Exmoor currently rests with riparian owners whose personal legal interests may extend only to a short section of river or property frontage. Such owners and residents clearly lack the influence over sporting enthusiasts enjoyed by public bodies or the potential to use or obtain public powers. For the private individual there are considerable difficulties in identifying canoeists against whom to seek civil damages or injunctions as a last resort. In short, private owners have only a limited practical control over intrusive watersports, often amounting to no more than ineffective persuasion.

A better way?

More extensive, but nonetheless sensibly limited, voluntary access agreements should be achievable[x]. These would not need to be exclusive to Canoe England members, provided the canoeists' representatives were willing in good faith to promote compliance with agreed conditions.

The formula for progress, on paper at least, is simple. Riparian owners should continue to engage constructively with canoeing representatives and not unnecessarily withhold agreement to access where the interests of all parties and the environment are properly balanced. Canoe England, for its part, should recognize the existence of legitimate public and private interests other than those of canoeists. Finally, the responsible public bodies should be prepared to show purpose and leadership in the interests of the National Park in a situation that has the potential to run out of control.

Hopefully, by the date of publication, the authorities will indeed have shown a new engagement and decisiveness.

The author is a member of the Lyn Riparian Owners' Association

i See Attorney-General ex rel. Yorkshire Trust v Brotherton, House of Lords 1991 and "Living on the Edge", Environment Agency publication 2007.

ii See Rawson and Others v Peters, Court of Appeal 1972.

iii Including the River Exe and Tributaries Association and the Lyn Riparian Owners' Association.

iv Public statement, Canoe England, March 2009.

v Contrast such free access with the legal restrictions on angling. The annual revenue from anglers' rod licences alone (which do not confer any right to fish) was estimated at £25 million by the Angling Trust in 2009.

vi See obituary, Lord Sandford, The Times 23.1.2009.

vii The Salmon and Freshwater Fisheries Act 1975 protects spawning salmon and their redds in all rivers.

viii The Countryside and Rights of Way Act 2000 places a duty on public bodies to further the conservation and enhancement of SSSIs.

ix ENPA Canoeing Policy June 2008 and Report to Authority April 2009.

x Information about agreed canoeing access available from www.activeexmoor.com.

DUNSTER – PIONEERING SIMPLE, SAFER STREETS AND PUBLIC SPACES

B Hamilton-Baillie

Exhibition Road in Kensington has just been repaved and redesigned to create a new kind of street. Still open to traffic, it has become a low-speed, fully integrated single public space, designed to reflect and emphasize the grandeur and civic qualities of the great museums, university buildings and institutions that form its boundaries. This is the most ambitious example so far of "shared space", reconciling traffic circulation with a low-speed, pedestrian friendly civic street appropriate to its role as the unifying element in London's principal cultural quarter.

The relevance of Exhibition Road to Exmoor is not immediately apparent. But precisely the same principles are being applied in a pioneering set of proposals for historic medieval Dunster, and other settlements in Exmoor National Park. More modest and less celebrated than Exhibition Road, the ideas for Dunster nonetheless represent an equally significant opportunity to address the issue of traffic in the key settlements that define much of Exmoor's built environment.

Traffic, and its impact on the quality of life, is high on the agenda for most local communities. With ever rising volumes and growing dependency on motor vehicles in rural areas, most towns and villages have seen a gradual, relentless erosion of distinctiveness and quality as highway measures are installed in response to traffic pressure. Road signs, road markings, traffic signals, barriers and bollards illuminated under Colditz-style lighting are often assumed to be the inescapable price for coping with traffic and maintaining safety. For many residents and traders, the only measures available are more signs or markings, or crude traffic calming devices with their attendant roadside clutter.

The damage to streetscapes resulting from highway measures has important economic implications. Towns and villages can no longer rely on serving as centres for trade. These are shifting to out-of-town superstores or to the internet. In place of their role as distribution points, towns depend more on the quality and attractiveness of their built environment and setting in order to draw in visitors and investment. Qualities of place underpin the economy of Exmoor. The standardization and uniform character of the highway is sharply at odds with the vital need to retain the distinctive and memorable characteristics that attract people to the landscape and its settlements.

Dunster's medieval streetscapes are especially vulnerable to traffic pressures. Located alongside a major strategic highway, and straddling an important regional route, Dunster has to cope with significant flows of visitor and through traffic. Vehicles have to negotiate the tight bends and narrow dimensions of its convoluted street pattern, streets where the presence of pedestrians in the carriageway is inevitable. Parking and deliveries add more pressure. Gradually signs, road markings, yellow lines, signals and other traffic paraphernalia dominate the foreground. The delicate balance between the role of the street as both highway and public realm is, like the rural economy, very fragile.

A radical new approach to coping with traffic while retaining inherent qualities has been put forward for Dunster. Initiated by a well-organized working group as part of Project Dunster, and keenly supported by Exmoor National Park Authority, a set of initial proposals has been drawn up by us. This represents a very different way to deal with traffic that could bring hope and opportunities for many other places struggling to cope.

The proposals for Dunster, like those for Exhibition Road, start by removing all of the signs, lines and markings associated with the highway from within the boundaries of the village. Centre line markings and yellow-box hatchings disappear. In their place comes a simple paving language that builds on and emphasizes the history, morphology and context of the historic village to create a strong sense of place. Thus the Visitor Centre, the Luttrell Arms Hotel, the entrances to Dunster Castle, the Church forecourt, the Foresters' Arms pub and, most importantly, the famous Yarn Market building in the High Street are all employed to build a sequence of distinctive spaces that draw the driver's attention to the peculiarities of the village. Every detail uses behavioural psychology to slow speeds and to add a sense of intrigue and interest to the streetscape. Streets are designed to feel narrower than they really are, and to give emphasis to long-established connections and pedestrian routes.

Creating a slow-speed environment for Dunster involves a number of simple, subtle measures to create a contrast between the complex, shared streetscape of the village with the simple linearity of the higher-speed highway. Clear transition points at the entrances to the village are used to form definite gateways and emphasize the change in scale and circumstances. Thus for Dunster, the entrance to the main car park on Dunster Steep is given greater prominence to mark it out as an important transition from the heavily engineered junction with the A39. Likewise, at the northern entrance to the village, the forecourt of the Foresters' Arms is arranged to mark a clear threshold to the public realm.

Project Dunster's initiative was enthusiastically welcomed by a large number of local residents and traders. The ideas also prompted other parish councils to explore whether similar thinking might help tackle long-standing traffic issues elsewhere. Encouragingly, officials from Somerset County Council have been supportive, and the key principles are prompting a fresh look at rural traffic issues across the County. The Dunster initiative is not unique. Although more widely adopted in Denmark, Germany, Holland and Sweden, there are examples in the UK. Dorset County Council has developed a *Rural Roads Protocol* and a tool-kit for rural communities. In Hampshire, similar measures are being explored for villages bisected by busy roads. West Meon on the A32 has seen traffic speeds drop significantly through the use of simple measures such as the removal of centre lines and signs, and some simple place-making. The villages of Clifton in Cumbria and Seend in Wiltshire have successfully adopted similar principles.

At one level, the principles of shared space that underpin the Dunster proposals represent a return to simplicity. The initiative can be seen, at its most basic, as doing nothing more than discouraging further damage from insensitive traffic measures. Certainly there is much interest in the potential long-term savings for beleaguered local authorities in not having to maintain expensive and costly signals, signs, barriers and other bits of highway kit.

But the Dunster initiative goes further than merely stripping streets of ugly clutter and returning to a bygone age. The proposals suggest ways to take Dunster forward in ways that enhance the delights of its intricate and varied buildings, doorways and spaces. Whether it is the setting of the Yarn Market, the front door of the Luttrell Arms, the gates of the castle or just an interesting shop front, the street plans seek ways to create a foreground appropriate to the rich patina of such historic settlements.

This is a big change in the way streets are designed and managed. For many years, engineers and planners have sought to keep civic life and pedestrian activity strictly segregated - vehicular traffic had to be kept clear of the day-to-day world of people. Overbridges, underpasses, pedestrian crossings, signals, kerbs and barriers were the result. The idea of deliberately linking buildings and their activities with the design of streets is still a relatively new idea, and represents a challenge to conventional safety engineering. Shared space exploits our increasing recognition that drivers are hugely influenced by the clues presented by their surroundings – remove certainty and monotonous predictability, and all of us respond instantly to the peculiarities and ambiguities of place. The social protocols implicit in the public realm, as in a camp site or supermarket car park, are more powerful determinants of behaviour than legislation, rules and speed cameras.

It is difficult for a small community on their own to question conventional wisdom and pioneer a new approach to traffic in towns and villages. This is where a National Park Authority can play such a vital role in supporting pilot projects such as Dunster. Exmoor NPA are amongst the vanguard of national parks and Area of Outstanding Natural Beauty Partnerships in seeking a new relationship between highway design and environmental quality in the countryside, mirroring the changes to street design emerging from urban contexts such as Exhibition Road.

It is still too early to say for certain how Dunster's plans will develop. But already they have prompted a new awareness amongst communities in Exmoor that alternative means to address the realities of traffic are available. No longer required to beg overstretched highway authorities for odd bits of clumsy traffic calming or speed cameras, local residents are now beginning to gain confidence that special places can be protected and enhanced as part of a practical way to promote lower speeds and civility, and to reconcile people, places and traffic.

BRIAN PEARCE: A RICH LEGACY

R Thomas

Exmoor has lost a true friend: a person who has devoted much of his life to exploring its hidden gems, understanding its history, communicating to a wide audience the interrelationship between nature and people, inspiring others to see its beauty in all seasons ... and so much more.

Three aspects of his legacy stand out.

First, Brian had an encyclopaedic mind and through his prodigious writings has left us with deep knowledge of Exmoor. From the Exmoor Review alone, which he edited in the last decade, articles range from discussing the theories that inspired the hymn " All things bright & beautiful" with reference to the strong Exmoor tradition of Dunkery or Grabbist Hill being the "purple headed mountain" to a review of Exmoor's changing landscape and history of the Exmoor Society.

Second, Brian was a an educator determined to pass on to others both his knowledge and love of Exmoor in many ways including walks, talks, field studies, worksheets, slides lectures and articles. In the 2010 Exmoor Review, he wrote about the importance of outdoor education and residential experience. He remembered his own stay at St Mary, Lyncombe, sleeping under the stars when it was just a platform with no walls or

roof. He said "It was so cold that a pool of ice under my sleeping bag never melted, but it was beautiful. And it was so tranquil — I spent a week there on my own walking the surrounding moors, and never seeing a soul the whole time. My love of Exmoor grew through such experiences."

Third, Brian was an artist who through his photography captured much of the richness of Exmoor life and inspired people to look more closely at its beauty. National recognition of his ability came when his photograph of Watersmeet, taken from Wind Hill looking across Chiselcombe was chosen to be a postage stamp in February 2005. Royal Mail thought that it was like looking down on a tropical rainforest which Brian said was appropriate because "Watersmeet is one of those special parts

Chiselcombe, Exmoor
South-west England
57

of Exmoor where you can actually imagine what the prehistoric landscape was like." And nobody will forget the front cover of the 2010 Exmoor Review with an Exmoor pony in the Valley of Rocks — a fitting tribute to his multifaceted talents.

Exmoor, indeed, has lost a true friend but one who has left a rich legacy not only to the Exmoor Society but to all of us who are moved by this place. Brian: writer, educator artist and friend.

ALL IMAGES COURTESY ELAINE PEARCE

THE CHELSEA GARDEN

S Head

Early in the morning of Tuesday 25th May 2010, we learnt that our Chelsea Show Garden had won Gold. That was shattering enough news for the group of beginners who had worked for three years to make the garden happen, but we also learnt that the garden was awarded Best in Show for the Courtyard Garden category, a triumph for designer Christina Williams and the Two Moors Festival.

But rewind a moment – why had we created a little bit of Exmoor and Dartmoor in the heart of London? It started back in 2007, when Penny Adie, Artistic Director of the Two Moors Festival had a crazy idea. The Festival began in 2001 in response to the Foot and Mouth epidemic, to bring some cheer to devastated local people, and to encourage tourists to come back. Since then, the Festival (a registered charity) has gone from strength to strength, bringing the very best music and young musicians to the South West, and constantly pushing the frontiers. In 2006 it commissioned the opera *"Tarka the Otter"*, designed like Britten's *"Noye's Fludde"* for a young and amateur cast. *Tarka* won the Best Stage Work prize in the 2007 BBC British Composers Awards. In the same year the Festival made world news when a long-saved-for second-hand Bösendorfer piano was dropped by the delivery firm. This disaster became a triumph when the Festival was presented by Bösendorfer with a brand new (and much better) replacement.

Penny's "crazy" idea was a show garden at Chelsea. With nearly 160,000 visitors, and a television audience averaging 3.2 million each evening, press and website coverage, Chelsea represented a colossal publicity opportunity for Exmoor, Dartmoor and the Two Moors festival. We would also be celebrating the Festival's tenth anniversary.

It took three years to reach Chelsea. Much of the first year was spent talking about the project, engaging supporters, and convincing ourselves it could be done. We met the ebullient and inspiring Max de Soissons, Shows Partnership Development Manager for the Royal Horticultural Society who loved the idea and gave us the determination to succeed. The next stage was working up a design with Christina Williams, who lives on Exmoor, which she knows and loves. But this was no easy brief. We wanted clear references to Dartmoor and Exmoor, as well as to music and to the churches where we held concerts – and it had to be a beautiful garden. And all within a 5m by 4m space.

Our fundraising need was substantial, covering the costs of building a safe garden structure, planting, publicity, special features, transport, local specialists and accommodation in London. Managing the budget was the huge responsibility of Elizabeth Nixon. We did not want to "sell out" to a big commercial sponsor, who might unduly influence the design, so we raised all our funds locally. Lady Arran allowed us to hold a Charity Auction in the ballroom of Castle Hill at Filleigh. Substantial sums were also raised by people opening their own gardens. Rathbones Investment Management supported the project, and many local firms helped with gifts in-kind, most notably Barnstaple's St John's Garden Centre and Nursery. They supplied many plants and materials, and the indefatigable Liz Pile.

We finally knew the project was financially viable when Dartmoor and Exmoor National Parks each provided £5,000. Now all we had to do was persuade Chelsea to accept our design.

Although we had enormous help from the RHS, their regulations are very daunting. The Chelsea Flower Show Manual runs to 129 densely packed pages and there are up to 28 forms, the worst being the Health and Safety Form which is the most rigorous I have ever seen. But then came a real confidence booster.

Christina managed to persuade Mark Gregory to be our contractor. Only when we went to his office did we realise quite how lucky we had been. His wall was bedecked with medals, mainly it seemed Chelsea Golds. Mark's approach to all our concerns (including that Health and Safety Form) was – "Don't worry – I'll sort all that out". Of course, having Mark as our contractor must have given the Chelsea selectors the confidence that we would deliver.

In November 2009 our design was accepted, so we were now officially in the 2010 Show – cue for both joy and panic, because we had 187 days to get everything right.

As May drew closer, Christina and Liz were working increasingly hard to source high quality plants and materials. We engaged local people to build important design features. Richard Eastmond of Ivybridge in Dartmoor built the granite wall which spanned the garden, providing character and sense-of-place. Peter Warne from East Anstey laid the radiating Exmoor stone sets which surrounded the pool and were central to the garden. The beautiful willow arches representing churches, which framed the whole garden, were made by Windrush Willow of Exeter.

The build-up started on Friday 14th May. Mark Gregory's team laid the framework, then raised stout posts to support thick plywood shuttering which retained the soil at the back of the garden. The shuttering also protected the granite wall from the pressure of the soil if it rained. Then the root-pruned windswept hawthorn was craned into place, as were a massive granite cross and a granite gatepost. In went Richard's wall, a pool and waterfall, and Peter's cobbles. The willow arches were slotted into tubes, and we were ready for planting.

Christina and Liz planted the garden, together with Kate Davenport from Tiverton and Annie Prebensen of Molland. Christina's choice of planting was inspirational, and wholly suited to the moist moors and uplands. The rear and sides of the garden were bounded by tall Exmoor beech hedges, and the high ground behind the granite wall planted with rough *Molinia* grass, heather and whortleberry. The foreground "garden" section had a mix of textured green foliage, with ferns, *Alchemilla*, *Rogersia*, *Hosta* and tiny *Gunnera magellanica*. Flowers were all in the orange through cream to white range, with particular highlights being *Trollius* "Cheddar" and "Orange Princess", *Astrantia*, *Primula chungensis*, various *Geum* and *Aquilegia* "Lemon Queen". Against the dark beech at the back of the garden, a great burst of stark white *Hesperis* drew the eye from the foreground colour into the heart of the composition.

After that intense build-up the show week itself was one of the most exhausting but exhilarating experiences I have had – and I was only there for three days. The public loved the garden, and many asked about the festival and visiting the moors. The most gratifying moments were when you would hear a lady approaching saying something like "I say Rodney, *there's* the Music Garden" – so it clearly came over well on the television too.

What took ten days to create took only two to dismantle. Fortunately, the garden is about to enter another life, re-erected at the Calvert Trust Outdoor Centre near Blackmoor Gate on Exmoor, where we hope that it can be enjoyed for many years.

So was it worth it? Yes – I think it succeeded beyond our wildest hopes.
Was it hard work ? Not half.
Would you do it again? No way! – but there again, well, maybe...

Pony Branding

A Tierney-Jones

The autumn mist is down on Winsford Hill, this high slot of well-worn heather-coated moorland on the southern edge of Exmoor. It swirls and hurls itself about like a demented dancer, restricting visibility to less than 100 metres. In the opaque air, the twisted isolated shapes of lone trees can be glimpsed as well as several low-bellied equine shapes, their broad necks sloped downwards as they forage for food. The Exmoor Pony is abroad, a hardy and elusive animal that is as potent an image of the area as the red deer.

The Exmoor Pony is also one of the great successes of animal conservation, after having sunk in numbers in the early part of the 20th century; the depredations of the Second World War on Exmoor, especially military training, also affected the herds. Happily, the animal is in a healthier situation nowadays; there are several herds on the moor, numbering about 350 animals.

Autumn is also the time of the annual gathering, a time when these resilient survivors who have called Exmoor home since the Ice Age are rounded up and corralled by farmers. Even though the herds roam their own particular parts of the moor (or various commons), the Exmoor Pony is semi-feral by virtue of this seasonal gathering (they are managed but their instincts are wild). During the gathering, farmers who own the herds decide which ones will go back on the moor and the ones they will try and sell.

So it is a necessary thing. Inspections are carried out on foals while stallions are moved to a different common if it is felt necessary; meanwhile most of the filly foals go back on the moor, though their brothers leave it for good, either to be sold as riding ponies or sent to graze on conservation projects (in the past some have been destroyed but this is becoming rarer thanks to the work of the Moorland Mousie Trust up on Winsford Hill).

If you've ever seen this event, either on the day itself, or on film (Johnny Kingdom naturally featured it in his TV series), you would agree that it is something that has more than the touch of the Wild West to it. The sound of dozens of ponies galloping across the moor, their hooves beating out an insistent rhythm, horse-riders aiming to funnel them into a holding area. None get away — or do they? Stories are told of the odd stallion or mare that manages to evade capture. According to Val Sherwin at the Moorland Mousie Trust, 'there was apparently one mare who avoided the gathering for up to three years. On the day it would happen she would go far away and even hide beneath a hedge. They are intelligent beasts'.

The gathering is a tradition that spans centuries and is essential to maintain the health of the various herds, but there's also one equally traditional aspect of the event that is being questioned amid calls for it to be stopped. This is the hot branding of foals, a way of identifying their owners and which common they belong to, that occurs during the gathering. It's a way of marking the ponies, a practice that has gone on since the 19th century and is seen as essential, especially for the welfare of the animals. 'If I get a phone call about a damaged pony,' says Val Sherwin, 'the first thing I ask is what is the number. If it is a mare the number will tell me which stallion it runs with and where. I can then tell the farmer who knows the territory where to look.'

However, debate over the use of hot branding is starting to heat up. In short, branding is being called cruel and barbaric, an unnecessary and outdated form of identification that causes trauma to the animals. Will this turn out to be yet another case of the rerun of the battle between animal welfare and tradition, as we saw with many of the debates over hunting (though class envy also seemed to play its part)? Or will Exmoor — as it does with many things — go its own way? What are the issues that matter?

On the anti-branding side Cilla King is a forthright critic; she is part of People 4 Ponies, a pony welfare group based in North Devon, though she does insist that the group is not an animal rights organisation. 'Banning branding is the most important issue facing Exmoor ponies today,' she says, 'is it vital for the welfare of the ponies themselves. We are dedicated to the rehabilitation, training and re-homing of wild and traumatised ponies and have spent the last seven years working on a daily basis with animals that have been severely emotionally traumatised by identification procedures which include hot branding. We have seen, many times, the permanent emotional trauma that is caused when these procedures are carried with the most appalling associated handling methods on previously untouched semi-feral foals.'

King is not alone in her condemnation. The British Veterinary Association (BVA) and the British Equine Veterinary Association (BEVA) are dead set against the practice — Chris House, the chairman of the latter organisation said: 'we believe branding is done more for tradition than identification. Having seen videos of branding sessions, I believe it is not very suitable.' The RSPCA is also against, though they admit that they don't have an alternative suggestion for identification. Meanwhile the Scottish Parliament looks set at the time of writing to ban the branding of all equine animals. Alternatives for identifying the Exmoor Ponies including micro chipping or freeze branding, all of which it is claimed are much more humane.

Rex Milton farms at West Anstey and has two breeding herds of Exmoor ponies; one of them — Herd 23 — is amongst the oldest on the moor, with a line going back to 1818. This was when the Royal Forest of Exmoor was sold and Nicholas Milton bought some of the Exmoor pony stock and began keeping ponies on Withypool Common. He is also President of the Exmoor Pony Society so this is someone who can equally claim to have the interests of the ponies to heart. He argues that branding is necessary, though his reasons are more practical than stuck in some blind rut of traditionalism (as Chris House might like to claim).

'Branding is a necessary hardship that we have to do in a moorland situation,' he says, 'if I was breeding ponies in a lowland area where they were used to be handled then I would put a micro-chip in them. I will welcome a micro chipping on the moor when a reader is developed that can read from 25 metres. The Exmoor Pony Society has also had a look at freeze branding. A hot brand on a pony takes 30 seconds, while a freeze brand can last up to two to three minutes. We thought it the crueller option. The other issue that I would bring up is if a hot brand traumatizes a pony then what happens when a farrier puts a hot shoe onto a horse? The last thing we want to do is inflict unnecessary pain on an animal that we want to enjoy.'

Milton is supported in his view by Sue McGeever, the Society's Secretary, who makes the point that those who apply the brand have a strict three-year training. For her, there's another issue, that of handling the foals which up until the gathering are totally wild. 'Being handled is a new experience for them and like any animal they are not keen on being restrained at first. Even a foal born in a domestic situation will be wary of humans at first and it takes time to win their trust. If you look at BBC footage of branding at the Milton's you will see that once restrained, the foals normally stand still for the branding, which is over very quickly. It has been known for ponies to actually lick the handlers hand whilst being branded.'

However, People 4 Ponies remains forthright in its condemnation of the practice and Cilla King argues that banning branding would actually help pony owners. 'If hot branding, ear-cutting, notching and tagging were all banned and if people were prepared to be educated in handling procedures, farmers would achieve much better prices for their ponies and organisations such as ours may well become redundant — the very best thing that could happen to us!'

Like the ponies during a gathering this is an issue that will run and run.

EXMOOR PEOPLE

Molly Groves

An obvious choice for a portrait of a real Exmoor person was of course Molly Groves, with her tireless advocacy of Exmoor – in particular, the people of Exmoor. So committed and determined in fact, that to tell the truth we were slightly in awe (excuse the pun) as we drove deep into the very heart of Exmoor, past the famous Lorna Doone church of Oare, to her farm. Her directions were characteristically very clear. Up the steep lane, to a closed gate, which was hospitably opened. A flurry of friendly dogs welcomed us, with smiles all round. We passed through a little gate, and sat for a moment chatting in her sunny garden. Our fears were immediately proved to be totally groundless. We soon discovered shared interests and mutual acquaintances, almost every one releasing a cascade of amusing anecdotes. Molly was naturally in her element. We could have spent hours enjoying her personal warmth and good humour. It was with some effort that we remembered we had a set of questions to put to her.

When you were a child, what did you want to be when you grew up?
Anything that could keep me on Exmoor. That was all that mattered really. I'd have quite liked to have been a carpenter, but did a secretarial course instead, which gave me some useful skills. I worked for a Solicitor and enjoyed, and learnt a lot from, the court work at Minehead.

And what was your favourite book?
I loved Mary O'Hara's books. I followed the life of Flicka as a mare, then a mother who escaped, through My Friend Flicka, Thunderhead *and* The Green Grass of Wyoming. *I think I've still got them.*

Who's had the biggest influence on you?
Mrs Harry Rawle at Court Place. They owned a wonderful library I could visit, and read about nature to my heart's content. Even Sidney Tucker's personal diary, kept by his wife, which was kept in a safe. 'Mrs Harry's' father kept the staghounds at Burrow at one time. 'Mr Harry' had been a Prisoner of War of the Turks for two years after the First World War ended. When he returned, he retreated into nature. He'd talk eloquently and at length about the animals I too loved – birds, deer and foxes. There were tales about many a hunting adventure, such as Sidney encountering the stag on a cliff path...

What's your happiest memory?
Coming to live in this house. We regularly brought our four young children to stay with Fred and Mary Baker and their three children. We loved it. Even in the 1963 snow. We kept warm, with mattresses and blankets. When Fred and Mary got an alternative farm we were delighted that we obtained the tenancy and we could come and live here.

What's your favourite colour – and why?
Green. I love the green grass, the green of new growth, fresh green leaves.

Is the glass half full, or half empty?

Half full, of course! Everything works out eventually, I believe. Mother had a fund of quotations she used, one of which was 'If the Lord don't come, he sends'. Although she was very much a Christian, it wasn't so much a religious statement as one of her stock phrases. In fact sometimes she'd add 'and sometimes he sends some very odd help.' Well, something always turns up.

What makes you angry?
Injustice. I'll always stand up and speak out if I feel there's unfairness. I've got involved in several fights over the years, what with the tussle with the Church over the ownership of the local Rectory, and the Porlock Surgery threatening to move to Minehead and the Hunt Police meeting.

Tell us about something you'd really rather forget
I honestly don't think I've done anything truly bad. When I have done something I've regretted,

I hope I've always apologised – that's the main thing. It's important to do what you think is right at the time. So, nothing really I'd rather forget

Where would you best like to be right now?
Why, here, of course!

What present would you like for your next birthday?
(Molly sat for some time in silence before answering)
For someone to pay for a gardener for three whole days please. I've got three small great grand-children now, and I'm trying to make a Beatrix Potter style woodland garden for them to enjoy.

What's your biggest regret?
Not saying something important to a special person who died. Once someone has gone, you can never say or do that thing, you always meant to.

What have you done that you are most proud of?
I've been lucky. I started the County Gate Information Centre – in a caravan. One night it blew away. (Somebody cheeky said it wouldn't have if I'd been in it.) I so much enjoyed telling visitors about Exmoor, tales about Jack Burge, Dick French and other village characters…

(At this point, Molly launched into an eye-wateringly funny story about a local chap driving a lorry up Porlock hill, who was stopped at the top – and with difficulty prevented from sliding back down – by the Police, who gradually discovered no less than 28 serious faults. It hardly seemed necessary to ask our final question)

Please tell us a joke
What do you get if you pour boiling water down a rabbit hole?
Hot Cross Bunnies.

After tea, we left Molly reluctantly. We'd been entertained by a great raconteur, but it was her essential personal modesty that won us over. Here was a person whose first and last love was Exmoor, for whom just being there and appreciating Exmoor in all its aspects – the landscape, the flora and fauna, its history, the people and their work – was more than enough. Happiness is not about acquisition or possessions. Rather, it is about acceptance of what is good around us, standing up to be counted when the need arises, and enjoying the natural world and where you are – in particular, people, friends and family.

UNDERSTANDING POLICY IMPACTS UPON HILL FARMING IN EXMOOR

J Dwyer

Researchers[1] from the CCRI have been studying the influence of current farming policies and, in particular, the existing and potential role of the Rural Development Programme for England (RDPE) on hill farming in Exmoor, and in the Forest of Bowland. This is part of a 3-year EU-funded project called RuDI (Rural Development Impacts) investigating policy effects across all 27 EU member countries (see www.rudi-europe.net). The key questions were:

1   How well is current RDPE policy supporting beneficial land management through farming, and how might proposed changes to upland support schemes be likely to affect this in the future?

2   Are there other ways, using this funding, which might work better?

Using all sorts of approaches, including statistics from Defra surveys and local research, we set about examining how farms have changed over the past ten years. We interviewed in depth a dozen contrasting farmers in each of the two upland areas to find out how policies had changed their farming practice, following this up with well-attended workshop feedback and discussions. Full results will be presented at a Defra-hosted seminar later in London, but here is a brief summary of the findings.

$$\boxed{1}$$

We found that the traditional inter-linked management of hill farming systems, where the moorland, inbye and better land on each farm would have been managed as a single enterprise using hardy breeds of sheep and/or cattle, is breaking down. Decoupled Single Farm Payment, entry into agri-environment schemes (both ESAs and now HLS), and the application of modulation are all partly responsible. Biosecurity policies in response to the outbreaks of foot and mouth disease, and especially in Exmoor, bovine TB, have also contributed.

Increasingly, moorland is now managed separately from the commercial element of the farm business, which is concentrated upon more intensive management of in-bye and valley bottom land. Moorland grazing is often achieved using ponies or hardy breeds of cattle, but these enterprises are separate from the sheep and beef-rearing on the lower hill slopes. Former upland dairying is in decline and there has been a loss of smaller 'starter' unit holdings from these areas as many farms have become larger, in order to survive.

These changes have also reduced the number of people working on hill and upland farms. The benefits of Agri-environment schemes, such as their contribution to the land-scape, and providing winter work, have not prevented increasing 'zoning' of these hill landscapes into either 'special areas' (moors and wet/hay meadows) managed exten-sively and mainly for conservation or environmental purposes, and 'other areas' managed intensively for agricultural production. This has helped neither local land-scapes nor biodiversity. Nor is it liked by the farmers themselves, weakening their sense of identity as 'true hill farmers'.

The current economics of hill farming are the reason. Many farms have some form of diversification to bring in extra income, and most are heavily dependent upon the various policy support payments. Whilst all the farmers that we interviewed were involved in agri-environment schemes, few had received support or advice from the economic 'half' of rural development programmes. Thus their business strategies have mainly evolved independently, coping with changing economic circumstances as they arise.

Some would argue that the hill farming system, as seen here, is no longer economic. Its survival is dependent upon external income. Can we go on like this?

Farmers feel alienated and misunderstood by policy makers at all levels. Whilst many farmers recognise and appreciate supportive attitudes among some advisors, this contrasts strongly with what they think about schemes' design and delivery. This lack of trust and credibility is likely to undermine RDPE achievements. Time and again, we heard that agencies were too distant, too concerned with their own targets and unable or unwilling to work together with farmers to flex the system to farmers' best advan-tage.

2

Future options for enhanced policy design
The main problem with current policy is the lack of joined up working between envi-ronment and farm business elements. So environmental schemes risk not delivering the intended environmental goals, with farm business changes working in the opposite direction, as farmers seek to cope with current and future challenges.

In future, if government policies under both CAP pillars could be based upon a more integrated view about what they are seeking for the uplands, and how to achieve this, a different approach might be possible. This might involve:

- more emphasis upon successful and sustainable business models for hill farming. This means more emphasis upon using the range of measures in axis 1 and 3 of RDPE to boost hill farming prospects, with investment in training, research/experimentation, advice and collaborative activity and exchange, as well as adding-value strategies;
- providing more explicit support for upland culture and communities, in order to enable resilient environmental management systems to develop which have the full

support of the people farming the land – using axis 3 and 4 measures to help local farming communities to recognise and maintain what is important to them;

- a new element of financial underpinning from the mainstream support systems, recognising that as modulation proceeds and decoupling and CAP reform increase the exposure of marginal farms to national and international competition, their case for public support to maintain the viability of the business, not simply to pay for additional environmental goods, increases. There are several ways that this could be provided. It could come from a new 'Less Favoured Area' (LFA) payment, coinciding with a planned new definition of LFA at the EU level. Alternatively, it could come from new payments targeted at the long-term sustainable provision of 'ecosystem services', through a mechanism that is not linked to the 'income forgone' model of agri-environment. It could also come from a shift in the targeting of SPS decoupled aid, for example by reducing the differential in payment rates for the three land categories for SPS. Reducing the SPS differential between SDA land and other land is an option, while for moorland, because the existing differential in payment is so large, it might be better to offer a tiered rate according to the total area of moorland claimed for, to provide greater support to those businesses managing smaller areas of moor, helping discourage the further enlargement of moorland units.

Future options for enhanced policy delivery

The study also makes a case for a new approach to economic and social regeneration in upland farming areas, to ensure that this develops in harmony with key environmental goals, as well as contributing towards them.

The RDPE must develop a more territorially-focused and multipurpose policy for sustainable rural development in the English uplands, so that a full range of measures – economic and environmental – can be applied in a more co-ordinated, accessible and indeed holistic way. This has to be tailored to each distinctive upland area, to be sensitive to those whom it targets, in a much more transparent and responsive way. There must be a stronger dialogue drawing farmers and agency officers together and, over time building up trust.

A policy process like this can build social capital, institutional trust and a higher commitment to achieving policy objectives - all of which will enhance positive policy learning for all concerned, as well as supporting the objectives and values of local stakeholders.

EXMOOR

by Emily Morrish

A deer and her foal
Step into a pearly shaft of moonlight
Mist starts to shroud the valley,
And far away,
The lonely hoot of an owl
Shatters the silence.

Dawn is breaking,
And a cloak of fog lies over the fields
Like a silver blanket.
It is quiet, but the first of the dawn chorus
Is starting to strike up.

I take off my socks and stand in the stream.
The crystal shallows lap at my feet
Like a cold but
Friendly dog.
Minnows flit among the pebbles,
Avoiding my net.

I sigh. One day,
All this would be gone,
Just like Jan Ridd's footsteps
Leading away
Over the moor

FROM BARROWS TO BURNT MOUNDS

R Wilson-North

Exmoor's moorlands and heaths contain some of the finest archaeological remains in southern England. There are many features, and even whole landscapes, which survive from early prehistory between 8000 and 3000 years ago. They form an unusual and precious survival in a country which is increasingly losing the evidence of its past. The round burial mounds and standing stones of the Neolithic and Bronze Age periods have become iconic features of Exmoor itself. They have not only come to define how we view Exmoor's distant past, but even contribute to the general character of the moorland landscape. Since the 1890s these magnificent monuments have been increasingly appreciated, with statutory protection now afforded to many of them.

However, in the last two years a number of chance discoveries along with programmes of solid archaeological fieldwork and research are challenging the traditional view of Exmoor's prehistory. These insights and discoveries are the reward of patient and diligent research – and some luck - in a landscape which does not give up the secrets of the past easily.

The pace of change in our understanding of Exmoor's past has been fuelled by the discovery of thousands of previously unrecognized sites through the work of the National Mapping Programme (2007 to 2009) funded by English Heritage. Over 12,000 air photographs have been examined and in excess of 2000 new sites were found. One of the first and most striking sites to be identified was the hilltop enclosure on Little Hangman above Combe Martin, which has defied categorization and forced a re-assessment of all the other prehistoric enclosures across Exmoor.

A new episode in our study of Exmoor's moorland past is the discovery of a series of hunter gatherer sites dating from the Late Mesolithic period around 8000 years ago. Ten years ago the only confirmed site on central Exmoor was at Hawkcombe Head above Porlock. Excavations by the University of Bristol and Exmoor National Park Authority from 2002-4, which continues, has led to the confirmation of a further five sites stretching westwards as far as Farley Hill on Brendon Common. We are now forced to recognize that the moorland was well used by hunter gatherers, who presumably hunted the deer in what was then a well wooded upland with abundant springs which these small hunter bands seemed to favour.

More tantalizing is the strange and elusive rectangular enclosure east of the Chapman Barrows. Discovered in the 1970s by the studious observer and utterly indefatigable Hazel Eardley Wilmot, it was later discounted by other fieldworkers as an area of peat cutting. Two years ago it was 'rediscovered' by Jeremy Holtom whilst completing an agri-environment scheme survey. I confirmed the archaeological validity of the site – that it was not peat cutting but much more ancient. I was nevertheless perplexed by its form and location. There are no parallels on Exmoor, so what could this feature be?

Several archaeologists have now visited the site and surveyed it, and the closest parallels from further afield seem to raise the possibility that it is a Neolithic mortuary enclosure where corpses were excarnated – left exposed to decompose – between 5000 and 4000 years ago. Further work is clearly required to confirm the date and purpose of the enclosure, but its location between Chapman Barrows and Longstone support its suggested role in a highly significant burial and ritual landscape.

Over the last few years Dr Mark Gillings and Dr Jeremy Taylor from the University of Leicester have been working on the remote moorland around Pinford and Lanacombe to investigate Exmoor's well known stone settings. These groupings of little standing stones are probably around 4,000 years old and are a unique feature of Exmoor – in other words they are not found anywhere else. The aptly named 'Exmoor Miniliths Project' has been carrying out fieldwork and excavation to examine the settings themselves but also to reveal the landscape in which they were built. Although the stone

Survey work in progress on the burnt mound in Hoccombe Combe

settings are often found in splendid isolation, the project has started to show that they may in fact lie within a busier landscape of prehistoric fields, settlements and other sites, mostly now too slight to be seen on the surface. The settings therefore may be the tip of the archaeological iceberg and a clue to a much richer, contemporary, historic landscape which lies buried just beneath the surface of the peat.

In November 2009 whilst taking a short cut, with Christina Williams, back to Brendon Two Gates from Badgworthy Water in a thoroughly horizontal, unrelenting, westerly downpour, I stumbled on a 'u'-shaped mound in the remote Hoccombe Combe. Lying on the flood plain close to a streamlet, the mound was clearly archaeological, and could not be explained by recent activity in the landscape…it 'felt' prehistoric. The distinctive 'horseshoe' shape and its proximity to water put me in mind of Bronze Age burnt mounds which I had encountered elsewhere in the British Isles. Because of the strong Irish distribution of these sites – there are 20,000 in Eire and very few in England - they

often carry the Gaelic name 'Fulachta Fiadh' – 'cooking places of the warrior hunters'. Burnt mounds are usually Bronze Age (2000-700BC) and have no definitive single purpose. They are thought to be associated with communal cooking, brewing, dyeing or leather tanning. Another more appealing but perhaps less plausible suggestion is that they are prehistoric sweat houses or saunas. Whilst there is something surreal in imagining the prehistoric inhabitants of Brendon parish sharing a sauna on the moor, I am reluctantly forced to side with the cooking and brewing school of thought, but remain convinced that burnt mounds may have served different purposes and that even individual mounds may have been used for a range of functions over their lifetime. Whatever the case, these sites somehow bring us closer to the lives of these people than even the standing stones and burial mounds.

As is so often the case with archaeology – and indeed the historic landscape of England as a whole – there is some degree of reassuring predictability in it. Burnt mounds fall into this category of predictability and to explain how that is so, it helps to envisage how they came about. In the Bronze Age, rectangular pits were dug close to watercourses and were lined with timber or stone and then sealed with clay. Water from the river was then poured into the pit and stones heated on a nearby hearth. The heated stones were emptied into the water and by these means 100 gallons of cold water can be boiled in 30 minutes – as has been confirmed by recent experiments in Ireland. The heated water could then be used for a number of purposes, on which the archaeological record remains largely silent. Once finished with, the stones were discarded around the pit thereby creating the distinctive 'u'-shaped mound. The shallow pit quickly silts up and is no longer visible on the surface.

The Hoccombe Combe site meets all the criteria of a burnt mound, but it was necessary to establish whether the stone within it was actually burnt. Geophysical survey, including gradiometry - which records the magnetic 'signature' of the ground - was carried out in February 2010 and has confirmed that it is indeed composed of burnt stone. It may come as a surprise that this is the first burnt mound to be found on Exmoor. Given their rarity in England, this site is therefore nationally significant. Moreover, it also forms part of a change in our perception of Exmoor's past and a redefinition of what Exmoor's prehistoric moorland archaeology actually is.

As I write (April 2010), Exmoor has endured two harsh winters which have flattened the moorland vegetation, especially the rampant bracken which increasingly spreads across the moor. Now a prolonged dry spell has slowed the spring growth. Taken together these factors have ensured that the moor is almost denuded of vegetation cover – it is an archaeologist's dream, and has not been so laid bare within the last 20 years. More archaeological sites are being revealed on an almost daily basis.

Whilst there is an inherent excitement in finding further examples of known types of sites, there is much greater significance in the discovery of types of sites that we have not so far encountered on Exmoor – like the mortuary enclosure, hilltop enclosures and burnt mound. In a sense we are beginning to see a different moorland archaeology; you could describe it as being a more fine grained view of the landscape brought about by a more zealous and rigorous attention to the moorland. Whatever the case, we are gradually moving the archaeological goalposts, and at this stage we don't know where it will lead us. I am put in mind of RH Worth's exhortation at the end of the 19th century to 'zealous and discreet archaeologists' that the antiquities of Exmoor have never received the attention they deserve. The lesson of this journey of discovery should serve to remind us all that, no matter how well we think we know this enigmatic and compelling landscape, it still has so much more to tell us about the people who lived here between 8000 and 3000 years ago. As these recent archaeological discoveries are made, the significance, appeal, attraction and interest of Exmoor's moorlands grow with every passing day.

The Bronze Age cist revealed by excavation on Lanacombe in 2009

Alfred Vowles Prizewinners

Heritage Category Commended – And the Running of the Deer (M Julian)

Overall and Landscape Winner – On the banks of the River Barle near Tarr Steps (R Yardley)

Landscape Category Commended – Looking Towards Dunkery Beacon (K Hann)

Heritage Category Winner – Clapper Bridge, Upton (J Rowlandson)

People at Work Category Winner – Working party at Dunster Castle (M Julian)

People at Work Category Commended – Glass Blower (P Leather)

CONFINEMENTS

by Molly Goodland

She is sway-backed and big-bellied
shifting her weight on tired legs.

Is it the pain that flattens her ears
or the memory of pain, brought close
by the sleek ungelded one, her last foal,
confined in the next paddock?

When the foaling starts his wild galloping
sends clods of dark earth falling.

Coming at last to a sliding halt
he watches as his mother reaches down
to her starred and gawky new-born,
already struggling to find his feet.

WHY DO I WRITE ABOUT EXMOOR?

P King-Fretts

We asked Paddy King-Fretts to tell us why he writes about Exmoor. This is his reply.

Well…it all began a very long time ago when, soon after the war, my parents bought Sandyway Farm, high up on the western edge of the moor. Back then the King was still on the throne, Churchill had yet to be re-elected and the Korean War still to be fought. Life up there was hard. No electricity or piped water, we had to generate our own. The farm 'tractor' was two horses and our car, as such, a WWII jeep that had seen service as a gun tractor. We killed our own meat, mother made most of our clothes and almost all our food. Yet it was a wonderful life. For me, however, just eight and older than my siblings, it was initially a strange existence. Too young to be given responsibilities, I was too old to be ignored so my parents gave me a pony, a gun and a dog, opened the front door and pointed.

In those days the heights of Exmoor were empty, little of the land had gone under the plough and many minor roads were no more than pitted tracks. For me, however, it was paradise and day after day I roamed alone, sometimes on horseback, sometimes on foot with gun in hand. About a mile away there lived another family and it was their son who taught me to tickle for trout, to gaff salmon and to stalk game. But mostly I was on my own. Soon shooting and fishing, with or without permission, and hunting with local packs became second nature. By the time I was ten I knew the moor well and the wildlife that lived there. I could navigate for miles in all weathers, select the best routes across difficult or boggy terrain, and understand what was happening around me by watching farm stock and the natural world. I had become a child of the moor and life in the wild had stamped its indelible mark. Later, as a soldier, I was to benefit time and again from what I learned up there as a youngster.

Back then the old men of the moor would talk about the Knights – Frederic, whom several had known personally, and his father John who had bought Exmoor from the Crown back in 1818. After a day shearing or docking, or working the horses in the hay meadows, I would listen spellbound as they recounted tales about how the moor was tamed, about the dramas and the incredible hardship, about how folk lived and often died in those far-off days. They spoke about village life as it was when Withypool, Molland and Exford had their own cobblers and thatchers, about village fêtes and gymkhanas and how visitors ('foreigners') were regarded by those who lived here. Exmoor, in those days, was a world quite unlike today where, for so many, it has become a rich man's playground.

Time moved on and at seventeen I left home. Then, after more than thirty years as a soldier I moved on again, this time to run a holiday business in France and it was there that my writing began. I had always been told (often bluntly) that writing was not for me. Stick with the sword they cried, and leave the pen to others. Yet it was in France where we took guests into our beautiful home near Toulouse that people told me I had to write about our seemingly idyllic life. Excuses fell on deaf ears and eventually I tried my hand. Months later I showed my efforts to a friend who, years earlier, had written about our French adventure in *The Weekend Telegraph*. Suzanne tore into me, pulling me to pieces and pointing out time and again the worst of the horrors. But suddenly she turned, rapped the table hard and told me that, in spite of all she had said, she found in my writing a style that people would enjoy, even pay to read, and that I had to persevere. But never forget, she instructed, the secret to any half-decent piece of prose is that it has to be polished and polished and polished again.

A year later *To France – with Love!* appeared and fared respectably well, selling out then selling out again until suddenly the publisher went bust, taking all my hard earned royalties with him. However, life moved on once more and I returned home. Having caught the bug, I vowed to press on and one day a chum of many years chanced by. Bruce Heywood and I had known each other since our teenage years and as we sat in the garden with a glass of wine he asked if I had ever considered attempting a biography. The life and times of Ernest Bawden, his great uncle, was perhaps a tale worth telling. The great huntsman was a legend in his own lifetime but I had better get on with it for there were still those around who had hunted with him. *Staghunter* was fun. I knew my Exmoor, I knew my hunting and many of the Bawden family. Research was fascinating, especially as his son Percy, now ninety-five, was still with us. Remembering Suzanne's advice about polishing hard, I took the manuscript to a number of those whose judgement I respected and begged them to read it with a critical eye and sharp pencil. *Staghunter* appeared in 2005 and sold out. It was reprinted and sold out again.

Biographies are relatively simple, for one must stick to facts. The boundaries as to what one can and cannot say are clearly defined. As long as the research unearths enough of interest it is a matter of assembling the material in such a manner that will please the reader. However, try as I might, I could not find another subject and, as I wanted to continue, I decided to try my hand at fiction. But a novel is so different. Unbelievably more complicated, one has to, in the first instance, find a suitable plot – a story that is going to hold the reader. Then there have to be the sub-plots. Then come the characters, the dialogue, the scene setting and everything else. Not easy! One of the cardinal rules about any writing is to know your subject well: thus I turned again to Exmoor, this time to the wartime years, which were similar to the Exmoor I first knew.

The story of Larkbarrow is well known. A Knight farm, it was built early in the nineteenth century in a remote and beautiful spot near the head of the Doone valley. During WWII the inhabitants were forcibly evacuated to make way for an artillery range when the old farmstead was shelled almost to destruction in the build up to D-Day. Later, in the early fifties, we used to picnic there when the house was still standing. I remembered it well and could imagine the heartache and pathos surrounding the departure of the inhabitants and the death of the lovely place. Here, then, was my story, this time a romance but a story which, if I could tell it well enough, might strike the right chords. *Larkbarrow – a story of Exmoor* first came out in 2007 and was re-printed a year later.

So, what next? Since boyhood I had studied the story of the Knights and their exploits. Without doubt the greatest story of Exmoor in modern times, it has been well documented yet there has never been a personal account – the story told by somebody who was there. And so I decided to do just that, tell it through the eyes of somebody who had grown up with the Knights. My trilogy *Jack Tucker of Exmoor* took several years and is indeed based on that great story. In Part One *The Wild Red Dawn* the reader meets Jack Tucker as a young boy when his father, Lionel, is killed at Waterloo. Jack and his sister Emma are sent across the moor to work for John Knight, Emma in the kitchens and Jack in the stables. It is not long before Jack meets the little boy, Frederic Knight. He, Frederic, is younger yet they become devoted, lifelong friends as I portray in Parts Two and Three, *Softly cries the Curlew* and *Neither Hope nor Fear*. I based my story on all I knew about the Knights with the young Jack behaving much as I did in my own childhood out on the moors. It is, I hope, a tale that both captures the imagination and allows the reader to get a feel for what it was like living high up on Exmoor, often with nothing more than the cry of wild birds and occasional glimpses of ponies and deer for company. It is the moor I knew as a boy and I have written about it in the hope that I can pass on a little of what life was like in bygone times.

My latest book *Night of the Octopus* is based on my experiences in the S.A.S and a recent Top Secret operation: for certain, a very different story.

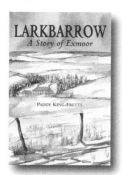 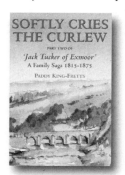 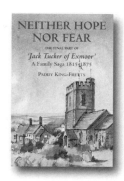

Most of the books mentioned can be purchased direct from Ryelands, Halsgrove House, Ryelands Industrial Estate, Bagley Road, Wellington, TA21 9PZ.   www.halsgrove.com Tel: 01823-653777, Fax: 01823-216796, email: sales@halsgrove.com

NIGHT IS RIGHT

T Oliver

When I was a child we lived on the edge of Exmoor in what was then the vicarage at South Molton. The house had a very good view into the moor. In late 1973, Comet Kohoutek became visible in the night sky over England. This was long before Comet Hale-Bopp soared majestically past the earth in 1997. My parents, taken in by the initial expectation that this would be the comet of the century (alas, it wasn't) spent some precious time looking for it and one night thought they'd found it, low in the dark Exmoor sky. Next morning they checked, lining up a mark they'd made on the bathroom window, recording where it had been. They were a trifle disappointed to see that what they'd thought was a spectacular Oort cloud comet (it was actually a Kuiper Belt object; much less flashy) was in fact a large new building, lit up like a comet at night. But what a portent this non-comet turned out to be after all: an omen of the incontinent spreading of artificial light across our night landscapes and night sky. Nowadays, it's possible to see a significant proportion of our constellations replicated in golf driving ranges, street lights, and security flood lighting below the night time horizon.

The spreading of light, for miles across the countryside and up across the welkin is usually regarded as a form of pollution. Although some regard the domination of the night by artificial light as an unalloyed good, many can distinguish between the value of being able to illuminate places at night, and the equal value of containing artificial light within the place it is actually needed. There is a widespread recognition that night should follow day, now as in the past. External lighting at night can be exceptional, rather than part of a cumulative plan to bathe our nocturnal environment in artificial light. Excessive lighting can also be regarded as polluting because of the possible harmful effects on some wildlife species. Bats and moths are both potentially vulnerable to intense artificial lighting. The University of Bristol is currently undertaking a Bats and Lighting Research Project.

We have actually made our nights far brighter over the last 65 years. This is shown in the remarkable research published by the Campaign for Dark Skies, the British Astronomical Association and CPRE in 2003. Since the end of the black out in 1944-5, external lighting has steadily grown in extent, intensity, variety and duration. Electric street lights and then the lighting of major roads spelt the arrival of the now all too familiar orange sodium glare. Major infrastructure has been increasingly brightly lit, partly in the name of safer working conditions and partly in response to an increased desire for security from crime or even terrorism. Late night leisure has played a part: riding centres, golf driving ranges and all-weather, all-evening sports grounds all throw light of a daylight intensity far beyond the places where the action takes place. And recently, too, the availability of security lights at DIY stores and garden centres, has opened up a new front in the fight against the darkness.

Until a few years ago, technological advance was almost entirely at the expense of darkness. Energy became cheaper, its use uncontroversial, lighting more powerful, and installation more affordable in relative terms. A richer, apparently busier society, has wanted to stretch the active day far into the night, at home as well as out and about.

And the consequences? Much lighter skies at night in ever extending tracts of the landscape. Lighting which burns brightly all night, illuminating countryside far beyond and the night sky further still. An ever wider distribution of sources of bright artificial light, beyond the reasonably orderly boundaries of urban and suburban development which this country has mostly managed to maintain, thanks to the planning system. Which is where Exmoor comes in.

National Parks legislation recognised places with outstanding landscape qualities and the opportunities they offered for public enjoyment. But the pressures to which the countryside has been subjected since then have been far greater than most people contemplated in 1949. Amongst these has been the degradation of rural night and the night sky. The unexceptional Norfolk countryside through which the otherwise bluff Parson Woodforde shrank from riding on a moonless night is now gently illuminated by the glow of Norwich and some nearby rural enterprises and bypasses. But Exmoor, deeply rural and less inclined than many districts to defy the cycle of light and dark, has remained protected from sources of intrusive light within its own boundaries. This is part of the specially tranquil character of the moor which is so effectively articulated by the Park local plan. The continued recognition of this quality is vital to the future distinctiveness and identity of Exmoor. The Park Authority has good local policies: LCN2 on the control of artificial light in new developments and TR8 on lighting associated with transport facilities are clear and to the point. These policies should be retained in any review of the local plan, if effective control of light pollution is to be maintained.

Intrusive light can be thrown from far afield, however. In this way, Exmoor is affected from two very different quarters. The first and much older intrusion is from across the Bristol Channel from South Wales. The fiery glow of furnaces and other industry must have been visible from the Exmoor coast for far longer than most light pollution, and the bright lights of some of the South Wales resorts have been winking at Exmoor since before the war. The lights of South Wales have, as elsewhere, expanded and arcs of sodium climb up many suburban slopes, displaying more orange tone to the observer at Lynton or Porlock. But perhaps the lights of Glamorgan, separated from Exmoor as they are by miles of sea, can help Exmoor's spirit of place by emphasising the very different character of the two shores of the Bristol Channel. But the second direction from which the inkiness of the Exmoor night is tinted a paler, more insipid tone, is from the expansion of mainly urban development on the edge of Barnstaple, Tiverton and west of Taunton. An ill-contained drench of security and transport lighting soaks into the firmament above Exmoor.

The solution to this violation of Exmoor's night might be a special dialogue between the Park Authority and the local authorities which immediately surround Exmoor. This includes Devon County Council, the highway authority and thus the controller of most of the road lighting which can play such a part in dispersed light pollution. For example, I was taken aback a few years ago by the sodium oasis on the western outskirts of South Molton where new roundabout lighting has transformed the dark world of the old A361 that I recall from the 1970s. There is a statutory basis for this approach in Section 11a of the 1949 Act.

The hopeful thing is that there are tried and tested solutions. Road lighting, which can sometimes genuinely improve road traffic safety, can be achieved using what are known as full cut-off lights, which do not let light spill away from the road that needs to be lit. When road or street lights are renewed, the perfect opportunity exists to deploy new, less polluting kit. Laudable efforts to reduce local authority costs and carbon emissions have a perfect companion in the reduction of hours during which lights are switched on. And the intensity of street lights is often far greater than it needs to be; the luminescence equivalent to full moonlight is easily enough to show the way safely and comfortingly. The intensity of light is also an important consideration for private security lights. Whether or not security lighting does reduce crime (and there is very little evidence to suggest it really does), intense floodlighting apart from being very polluting and very expensive in energy, casts dark shadows which conceal far more than such lighting reveals. This is now commonly received wisdom. This matters, particularly in a very rural place, where often isolated farms need to make well-judged decisions about the effectiveness of their own security.

In many rural settlements, beautiful buildings are lit to celebrate their qualities. But alas, in being so lit, these very qualities are diminished. The light pollution which ensues is often particularly intrusive in an otherwise dark place. But the instinct is sound, places and buildings should be celebrated and shown. There need be no conflict. Churches, town halls and monuments can be lit softly and still show their fine architecture; they can be lit for a few hours in the evening, or they can be lit on special days, to create a sense of genuine occasion.

Lighting is a clever invention which adds greatly to our quality of life. But like anything, too much can be poisonous. Exmoor is a place as yet relatively untainted by profligate lighting within its boundaries. With diplomacy and application, surrounding communities may also be prevailed upon to be sensitive to this rare quality as well as benefiting themselves from restraint. The message should be that on Exmoor, night is right.

Book Reviews

EXMOOR ADDRESS BOOK
Photographs by Peter Hendrie
hb, 112pp, 2009, Halsgrove, £12.99
ISBN 978 1 84114 985 1

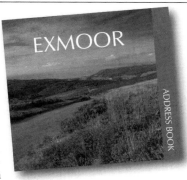

This beautifully produced address book from Halsgrove showing Exmoor in all its varieties, in all seasons, would make a much-appreciated present. Encountering the many Exmoor moods here illustrated turns the chore of chasing up an address into a pleasure, as one leafs through full-page high quality photographs ranging from beetling cliffs to Exmoor ponies, from iconic lines of beech hedge to wintry moorscapes.

A MARITIME HISTORY OF SOMERSET
Volume One: Trade and Commerce; Chapter Three
Philip Ashford
Somerset Archaeological and Natural History Society

Porlock Weir's quay and its associated trade development from 1420 to 1790 is masterfully described and superbly illustrated in this chapter. If this excellent essay is representative of the parent volume, The Review looks forward to studying and enjoying the latter. Meanwhile – along with all other books, monographs and academic papers received – this material is available in the Society's library for members' use.

NEITHER HERE NOR THERE?
The mining and transport of iron ore from the
Brendon Hills to South Wales 1825 – 1925
M H Jones & J R Hamilton
Exmoor National Park Authority
ISBN 978 0 9563674 0 2

A majestic pair of volumes from the ENPA Old Mineral Line project throws great credit on all concerned. This formidable academic achievement, drawing on all kinds of primary evidence, and wonderfully illustrated with maps, diagrams, plans, photographs, portraits and reproductions of letters, bills, advertisements and every kind of paper record offers hours of fascination to anyone with an interest in this subject, not to mention the area, and the people who lived and worked here.

But this is no dry documentation – not least admirable is the authors' success in bringing all this historical scholarship to life. Individual experiences (sadly only too often tragic) are sensitively described and reflected upon. Thus for example we are taken painfully graphically through the events following the lighting of the quill which would then splutter its unpredictable way towards the main charge…

> *'Complete darkness, rarely experienced on the earth's surface, becomes, underground, a very different, primordial blackness…'*

Even an initially casual reader will soon find themselves enmeshed.

No price is declared for these tomes whose publication was made possible by a grant from the Heritage Lottery Fund – a demonstrably worthy use of these moneys. Society members are not only welcome but recommended to borrow these heavy to lift, but difficult to put down volumes.

A YEAR ON EXMOOR
Adam Burton
hb, 112pp, 2010, Frances Lincoln Ltd, £16.99
ISBN 978 0 7112 2979 2

Adam Burton is an award-winning professional landscape photographer who has put together a fine collection of photographs of Exmoor, providing an excellent introduction to this most beautiful of national parks.

At the beginning of *A Year on Exmoor*, the author gives a brief summary of the moor's history, geology, geography and wildlife. Throughout the book, the captions which accompany each photograph are thoughtful and informative, particularly for visitors to the area.

The photographs convey the drama and diversity of the Exmoor landscape, ranging from remote moorland to spectacular coastline; from rolling farmland to picturesque villages; from endangered wildlife to rivers lined with beech and oak. Exmoor's changes through the seasons are imaginatively documented, capturing the ethereal quality of winter; the vivid colours of spring; the brightness of summer and the dazzling displays of autumn. Whilst the book concentrates, perhaps too much, on honeypots such as Watersmeet, the author's personal fondness of this stunning environment has been translated into a photographic collection of universal appeal.

Elizabeth McLaughlin

Near Alderman's Barrow Allotment
A Year on Exmoor

THE SECRET CAVE
Margaret O'Hara,
hb, 64pp, 2009, Rare Books and Berry, £7.95
ISBN 978 0 9557119 4 7

Margaret O'Hara has dedicated this charming and entertaining book to her grandchildren, three of whom are the main characters in a story which is set in the heart of Exmoor. *The Secret Cave* is a very up-to-date children's tale which has all the key elements of an exciting page-turner. There are lots of adventures when the three boys make a summer den and befriend a young Welsh dragon called Llewyllyn. The dramatic saga reaches a white-knuckle climax as wicked bank-robbers brandish their shotguns when accidentally discovered by our intrepid heroes. All of this is set against the backdrop of a family in which grandparents are clearly indulgent of their grandchildren, and yet who know just when to be educational, practical, firm and wise. The book is pure modern make-believe, rooted in good old-fashioned Exmoor values.

Elizabeth McLaughlin

FEEDING LADY WINIFRED'S CATS
Molly Goodland,
pb, 54pp, 2009, Rare Books and Berry, £7.95
ISBN 978 0 9557119 5 4

It may be helpful to know that this Molly is the same as Molly Richards, author of *Growing Wild on Exmoor*. For this book of poems too is much about the nature of Exmoor.

The poet writes simply and from the heart on many aspects of the moor. Flora and fauna – birds, all kinds of creatures from slow worms to Exmoor ponies, trees and the landscape itself – are all described graphically with a deep affection and lack of sentimentality.

There's a sense of humour too – you'll often find yourself smiling. Many of these poems are in blank verse, but the poet often chooses to use more traditional forms, when her verse bubbles with amusing rhymes, names such as the Snerdly-Bobs, and crazy situations. Above all, she can laugh at herself, as in her Old Age Cocktail (her own recipe).

So it's about much more than Exmoor. Proud to be a grandmother, Molly communicates deeply about families. The joys of childhood, coming to terms with changes in relationships, the acute and chronic pain of bereavement – indeed many of the ups and downs of life – are all dealt with here.

Throughout we are faced with an invariable honesty. Her own bleak times are confronted, along with loss, ageing and death itself. And if hope is not always be found, there is always a clear unflinching acceptance, often tempered 'with just the ghost of a smile'.

We are pleased to be able to print two of Molly's poems from this collection in this Review, and warmly recommend this book which manages to be nostalgic without sentiment, to delight in simplicity while recognising underlying complexity, and rewards many a re-reading.

CULBONE, OARE AND BRENDON REMOTE EXMOOR PARISHES	UNFORGOTTEN EXMOOR WORDS AND PICTURES FROM A VANISHED ERA VOLUMES ONE AND TWO	PORLOCK IN THOSE DAYS
Dennis Corner, pb, 64pp, £5.95	*David Ramsay, hb, 128pp,*	*Dennis Corner, hb, 96pp,*
Rare Books and Berry	*£9.95 each*	*£12.95*
ISBN 978 0 9557119 90 9	*Rare Books and Berry*	*Rare Books and Berry*
	ISBN 978 0 9557119 8 5	*ISBN 978 0 9557119 7 8*
	ISBN 978 0 9563867 1 7	

Four charming books from the Porlock publishers Rare Books and Berry celebrate the landscape and characters of this area.

With old photos galore – and some new colour pictures – and many an anecdote, any would make a lovely present for anyone interested in this part of Exmoor.

Dennis Corner is a well-known local author: historian at Porlock Museum, MBE for services to local history in Somerset, who most certainly knows his stuff. For example, read all about the use car manufacturers made of Porlock Hill – such as the Singer Car Company which drove a new car up and down the hill a hundred times non stop. It was christened the Porlock Model.

David Ramsay, a more recent arrival, has assembled a fascinating collection of reminiscences of Exmoor characters, alongside intriguing illustrations such as – Porlock Hill again – the water barrels by the AA box at Pitcombe Head, for replenishing boiled over radiators.

WEST SOMERSET IN THE NEWS
Jeff Cox,
hb, 160pp, 2010, Ryelands, £19.99
ISBN 978 1 906551 09 4

If you enjoyed the *Free Press* article earlier in this Review, here's the book itself – a handsome volume, beautifully set out, documenting events from cheap trips to Bristol on the fast sailing steamer *Iron Duke* (wind and weather permitting) from Watchet in the 1860s, to the seizing of a senior master of the hunt consequent to the Hunting Act in 2006, via the famous overland launch of the lifeboat, the first plane's arrival in 1914, evacuees, the building of Hinkley Point and the Jeremy Thorpe controversy. Well, that's just for starters…

'Many of the things chronicled in local journals may appear very small, but life is made up of small things' the author quotes Dickens. True enough, but somehow this wonderful book encompasses much more – we see national, not to mention international, history playing out through a local lens. Take a glimpse at some of the chapter titles –
1870s: Railways expand as turnpikes close.
1940s: Junkers, Eisenhower and a gift to the nation.

By selecting from the best stories of the *Free Press* over 150 years, often reproducing facsimiles of its text and pictures, Jeff has created a highly entertaining, amazingly informative and simply unput-downable history. I can't think of a nicer Christmas present.

OBITUARIES

BRIGID SOMERSET
1922-2009

Brigid Somerset, who died in November 2009, will be remembered by many members of the Exmoor Society as the loving and supportive wife of Guy Somerset who chaired the Society so ably for nearly twenty years.

Brigid was born in Oxford in 1922. She was brought up in an academic and clerical family, her father being the theologian and philosopher, Canon Leonard Hodgson, who was Regius Professor of Divinity at the University of Oxford from 1944 to 1958. She spent her early childhood in New York returning 'a right American gal!' before moving to Winchester where the family lived in the Cathedral Close and Brigid attended St Swithun's school. It seems unbelievable these days but she and her brother had access to a cathedral key and would creep into the ancient building after dark and play amongst the Norman arches.

Brigid trained at the Central School of Speech and Drama, became an actor and carried her equity card all her life. With the outbreak of war the School was evacuated to Exeter where she became a fire warden and saw the bombing of the city. After training she spent three years teaching at Downe House, Thatcham – not the happiest of her life – and on VE day was so determined to enjoy the day that she cycled the 28 miles over to Oxford to join her family for VE celebrations, cycling back in time for morning assembly.

She continued acting and teaching and then, on New Year's Eve 1948, at a party with Cambridge friends, she met Guy whom she was to marry. They lived for a while in London and then in Warwickshire and Adam, Jo and Honor were born. Guy's job involved much travelling and eventually, looking for a permanent home, they moved to Exmoor in 1973, living for a short time in Bilbrook before moving to Hoar Oak Cottage in Alcombe. Brigid had happy memories of bucolic family holidays spent at Leighland with a distant relative who was the rector there. Both Brigid and Guy were keen walkers and loved Exmoor and it was not long before Guy became fully involved with the Exmoor Society.

Meanwhile Brigid had her own entirely different interests and was fully involved in many areas of community life. She was, for instance, a long-serving volunteer with the West Somerset Stroke Club, took an active part in the life of the church in Alcombe and was involved in the local U3A Poetry and Literature Groups. Besides teaching for many years, Brigid was an adjudicator in Drama and Verse Speaking for the Poetry Society, the English Speaking Board, and the National Federation of Music Festivals. She was also appointed by the Diocese of Bath & Wells to travel all over the diocese advising clergy and readers on their preaching.

While living in Somerset she continued her acting career, sometimes being called on to take part in television productions: she featured in *Casualty* and in a BAFTA award children's series in the late 1980s, *Maid Marian and her Merry Men*, with Tony Robinson, where she portrayed a medieval hag with blacked-out teeth – a far cry from her more youthful roles on stage but she loved it.

When illness struck, Brigid had to abandon her career and began to write poetry encouraged by her fellow poets at Dillington House, Ilminster, and found she had a gift for it. A number of Brigid's poems have been printed in poetry magazines – and in the Exmoor Review and *Exmoor The Country Magazine* – and many have won prizes. In 2004 the Minehead Genge Press published a warmly-received collection of these poems, which vividly express Brigid's unique personality. Her publisher, Sue Lloyd, wrote of Brigid as a poet: "Amused, intelligent and perceptive, her range was wide: she could write wittily about human foibles and poignantly about old age and death; she was also responsive to natural beauty and several poems were inspired by her love of Exmoor." Many of her friends looked forward eagerly each Christmas to the poem which she sent as a seasonal greeting and these were collected and published by the Genge Press in 2008. Brigid continued to write poetry well into her eighties.

When Guy was disabled by a stroke, Brigid, in poor health herself, nursed him through his final illness until his death in 1996. Her last years in West Somerset were spent at Carhampton, where she joined fully in village life. She was a feisty, outspoken and highly intelligent woman who had a great capacity for making friends and loved entertaining. I remember wonderful parties in the barn at Hoar Oak Cottage while Pauline Bennett recalls that Brigid made "a mean prawn risotto and always enjoyed a small glass of whisky in the evening." She was very fond of her garden at Carhampton where she continued to entertain friends and visiting musicians performing at the Minehead and Exmoor Music Festival.

In her last years Brigid moved to Aberystwyth to be near her family, corresponding regularly with her friends in West Somerset and always eager to hear news of both Alcombe and Carhampton. She had always been independent and when she became ill it was irksome to her at first to have help, but then she took it in her stride and accepted and appreciated it.

In her tribute to Brigid, Sue Lloyd wrote: "One of Brigid's last poems, inspired by the death of an old friend, and entitled *Personal Walls*, has as its first line: 'A new person-shaped hole has appeared in my wall.' With Brigid's death, many of us will feel the same." We certainly do.

Hilary Binding

My thanks to many of Brigid's friends and family who contributed to this tribute.
Brigid's *Poems* and *Poems for Christmas* are available from The Genge Press. 01643 706461.
gengepress@aol.com

JOHN MILTON
1931-2010

It always seemed inexplicable that John had never been given a national honour, although he would undoubtedly have regarded the presence of so many hundreds of friends at his funeral as the greater reward. For John had a lifetime of public service, stretching back at least to his twenties when he became Chairman of West Anstey Parish Meeting, a position he still held when he died in post 54 years later. In between he packed in several careers worth of civic responsibilities: Governor and Chairman of West Anstey School; Governor of South Molton Community College, West Buckland School and Bystock Court at Exmouth; Chairman of the Exmoor Association of Parish Councils; and a founder-member of Mole Valley Farmers (born after a get-together

between John and fellow members of South Molton Round Table, and whose first merchandise, as John recalled, was a dozen buckets and a dozen pairs of Wellington boots). Above all as, first a member of the South Molton Rural District Council from 1969, when he took over from his father as a councillor, and then of its successor, North Devon District Council from 1974 until 1999, as member for the Bishops Nympton Ward. John was a distinguished councillor, serving as Chairman of Council from 1990 to 1992, not an easy position but which he filled with vigour and aplomb.

Sometimes a long list of public positions suggests seeking after office for its own sake, but with John you knew this was absolutely not the case. He did these things because he cared deeply about the area and about the people in it: and they in turn trusted him completely to defend their interests and to do the right thing for them. Nowhere was this more obvious than in relation to Exmoor – on, and on the fringes of which, John and his forebears had farmed for generations. John was appointed to the National Park Committee in 1974 and he served for 25 years. For some of that time he was Vice Chairman; were it not for the fact that until 1997 it had to be chaired by a Somerset County Councillor he would almost certainly have been its first native Chairman. As it was he did something probably even more important and certainly more difficult: he became Chairman of the National Park Planning Committee. In this guise he was to many people *the* public face of the Park, as planning is the part of the Park's activities that touches the Exmoor local most closely. John had to mediate between National demands on the one hand   and local needs, requirements and aspirations on the other, something he did conspicuously fairly but invariably with the benefit of any doubt being given to the genuine applicant.

One quickly understood that when John's fist grabbed his lapel, his thumb pointed firmly upward and he leaned back in his chair, you were about to receive words of wisdom – sometimes at considerable length, it has to be said: a friend once remarked that John could make two items fill an entire three hour meeting, and that was just the Apologies and the Date of the Next Meeting. But no one has ever written that wisdom has to be brief, and everyone learned so much from everything that John said. Sometimes John's advice was given less publicly, but no less forcefully. At least one Park Chairman was taken aside and told that on no account was he to rock the boat on hunting. And one new National Park Officer, whom John had helped to appoint, was gently commanded to move house, more or less immediately, to live in the Exmoor area. Everyone complied with these and other instructions because John was held in such respect and affection and because you always knew that he had only the best interests of Exmoor and the Exmoor people at the centre of his heart.

No man is an island, and John was the first to acknowledge that everything he achieved could not have been done without the gracious partnership of Hazel, and of Robin and Rex and in due course Karen and Banger, in running the farm and the considerable tourism business at Partridge Arms. It must have given John considerable pride and satisfaction that only a few months ago Robin was appointed to the National Park Committee to carry on the Milton tradition of service to the Exmoor that John loved so much, and which by the time of his death "Councillor" had become such an essential part of. John embodied the best characteristics of a true son of Exmoor: love of the land, support for its traditions (especially sporting ones), and care for your neighbours – which for John meant everyone from Bishops Nympton to Bossington - and it is greatly to John's credit that in his family he has such dedicated and able successors.

Steven Pugsley

MICHAEL DEERING
1926-2010

Michael Deering was born in Bushey in Hertfordshire in 1926, into a family which had prospered in the Thames lighterage business. An unhappy childhood was followed by the freedom of Reading University, where he studied electrical engineering and met his future wife Norma. A career in the electrical industry, latterly as Director and General Manager of Simplex Circulume , based in the North Midlands was successful but unsatisfying and so in 1974, Michael, Norma and the youngest of their four children, quit the "rat race". They moved to the Devon and Somerset border at Old Ways End, taking the shop and post office, and combining that with Norma's dressmaking business and Michael's photography.

Michael soon became known as *the* photographer for southern Exmoor. Rarely a week went by without one of his pictures appearing in the *West Somerset Free Press*, and over the years he did a significant amount of work for the Exmoor National Park Authority. People brought him pictures to copy, others commissioned new ones. Over the years he accumulated thousands of negatives. His burgeoning love of history and this amazing collection came together in the 1990s when he created the Exmoor Archive. Eventually housed in 36 meticulously arranged volumes, the Archive consists of over 1800 pictures with accompanying text, a fantastic resource for anyone interested in local and social history. There was so much material that when Michael came to compile a book, the difficulty was knowing what to leave out. *Exmoor In Sight*, a typically witty Michael title, was published in 1997 and is a fine testament to his wider achievement in preserving this precious corner of England's past.

Steven Pugsley

WILL IT BE WINTER?

by Molly Goodland

Will it be winter
when I join those souls
forever roaming about the moor amongst
the dead and dying bracken; seeking
always seeking, rain-lashed
or swirled and lifted in cold air,
scattered like invisible seed

or briefly silenced under a covering of snow?

And will it be soon when I follow
wild ponies and deer among frozen
tracks beside stunted trees, pointing
rime-thick fingers to the sky?

Will there be nothing but soft whispering
through the sedge, gentle keening?

If you might pass along
the paths we once walked, and feel
a fleeting otherness, lighten your step
and think of me, perhaps with just
the ghost of a smile.

ENPA Report

N Stone

Last year, the National Park Authority published a list of ten priorities for its work over the forthcoming twelve months. Looking back, we are pleased that all of the priorities have made significant progress and most have been achieved.

We set two priorities for the enhancement of Exmoor's special qualities – securing additional funding for conservation and lobbying for greater support for Exmoor farming.

Following a long and complex bidding process we were pleased to hear that Heritage Lottery Fund had agreed to provide £662,500 towards a three year Exmoor Landscape Partnership programme. The programme has been put together by a partnership of 12 organisations chaired by Rachel Thomas, Chairman of the Exmoor Society. There are 21 linked projects with an overall value of over £1.3 million and coordinated by a project team of five.

The programme emerged from the Exmoor Society's *Moorlands at a Crossroads* report in 2004 that highlighted the challenges of managing and maintaining Exmoor's moorland areas and reinstating their importance to farming, local communities and Exmoor's many visitors. This linked closely with the Heritage Lottery's three aims which are to **conserve** the UK's diverse heritage for present and future generations to experience and enjoy; to enable more people, and a wider range of people, to **take an active part** in and make decisions about their heritage, and to enable people to **learn** about their own and others' heritage.

The varied programme in the Exmoor Landscape Partnership reflects these three aims and includes the potential to create new jobs and apprenticeships in moorland management, volunteering opportunities, educational visits and outreach to communities living close to Exmoor but outside the National Park.

New resources for conservation have also come from South West Water who received the consent of the water industry regulator, Ofwat, to fund peatland restoration programmes in Exmoor and Dartmoor. By working with landowners and farmers to 'rewet' drained areas of peat, the aim is to help reduce the costs of providing future drinking water supplies by reducing the incidents of flash flooding in Exmoor rivers together with a reduction in soil erosion which harms water quality. Restored peatlands also help lock in carbon within the peat and, once a healthy new moss layer is growing again, will help lock in carbon from the atmosphere.

The SWW funded programme builds on the achievements of the Exmoor Mire Project that has succeeded in the past four years to repair peatlands on 300 hectares of moor in 17 locations in the National Park. This involved blocking of more than 50 km of ditches using 10,000 grass bales and 4,300 peat dams.

The partnership between the Exmoor National Park Authority and Forestry Commission has also continued to attract funding to Exmoor through the Exmoor

Ancient Woodland Project. Over the three years of the project we are on target to secure grant agreements worth more than £2 million to woodland owners to enable them to bring their woodlands back into favourable condition and management.

Similarly, through agreements with Natural England farmers on Exmoor receive more than £5 million a year to help farmers to maintain landscapes, wildlife, cultural heritage and public access in the National Park.

Support for the farming community is another priority for the National Park Authority and we have worked closely with South West Uplands Federation and regional organisations to lobby for future support for hill farming in the region. As well as securing the continuation of Environmentally Sensitive Area (ESA) conservation plan funding and targeting by Natural England of Environmental Stewardship funds to upland areas, we have also secured the commitment of the South West Regional Development Agency for a new Exmoor Hill Farm Project.

The Project employs three part-time staff based in Wheddon Cross led by a board made up of local farmers and chaired by Authority member, Professor John Wibberley. The project aims to help improve the profitability of livestock farming on Exmoor and increase access to grants from the Rural Development Programme.

Farming on Exmoor also received a boost from the start of the building of the new livestock market at Cutcombe. Close working between the livestock market, National Park Authority, Somerset County Council, Summerfield developers and Magna Housing Association brought forward plans for a new market plus business units and local housing. This scheme and the National Park Authority's role as planning authority, was commended in March 2010 when a visiting group organised by the Commission for Rural Communities visited Exmoor.

Other notable conservation achievements in the past years include the completion of the first phase of the West Somerset Mineral Railway project. The publication of the Victoria County History book *Exmoor, The Making of an English Upland* in June 2009 was also an important achievement in helping to introduce people to the rich history o the National Park.

We were also delighted at the Planning Inspector's decision to uphold the refusal of permission for two windfarm developments to the south of the National Park. Evidence was presented to the planning inquiry by Mid Devon and North Devon Councils together with strong support from the Exmoor Society and other local groups that clearly demonstrated to adverse impacts that the development would have on the setting of the National Park. The result was a favourable report that has helped to set an important precedent for any future proposals that may come forward.

Improvements to the public rights of way network in the National Park remains a high priority for the Authority with support from the Somerset and Devon County Highway Authorities. A sample survey indicated that 93% of the network met the national 'ease of use' standard and we are making good progress towards the target of at least 95% up to the standard by the end of 2011.

Ten major path projects were completed this year by the Authority's Field Services Team with 4,900 metres of path regarding, together with clearance of 149 windblown trees: production and installation 1,309 waymarker signs: clearance of 1,329 drains: 280 kilometres of vegetation clearance etc. etc.

A few other notable achievements during the year included support for 31 local projects through the Exmoor National Park Sustainable Development Fund and the organisation of 21 events across the National Park to ask for local views on future planning policies for Exmoor. Nearly 1,000 local residents attended the events and the comments and responses we received are now being brought together to help review and improve planning policies for the new Local Development Framework for the National Park to help look after the special qualities of *'Our Future Exmoor'* while enabling local communities and the economy to develop and prosper.

THE SPEECH OF EXMOOR

R Westcott

The very first Exmoor Review recognised the special qualities of Exmoor speech and the importance of its contribution to the uniqueness of Exmoor. John Coleman Cooke in his Chairman's Review made a strong case for cherishing and preserving the speech of Exmoor – along with the natural landscape.

'There are many forces today that tend to mould youth into one standard pattern. We hope that in spite of this trend, local traditions of speech, behaviour and belief will persist; that an Exmoor shepherd will not become interchangeable with a Durham miner, or a farmer's son with a barrow boy.'

He urged the Review to keep alive some of this 'differentness' of speech, as part of our appreciation of Exmoor.

In fact, over the years great efforts have been directed at just that. The Victorians took dialect so seriously that they compiled large glossaries of the various local vocabularies. Frederic Thomas Elworthy, member of Council of The Philological Society no less, published in 1886 a wonderful dictionary, which was nearly a thousand pages long. He had already compiled a grammar, which systematically works its way through nouns (particular emphasis on the various forms of plural), adjectives, multiples, fractions and distributives, prepositions, pronouns and verbs as intricately as Kennedy's notorious Latin primer. Picture a bewhiskered gentleman scholar, painstakingly noting how the locals spoke, and struggling to clarify the sounds…

'The most striking feature in the pronunciation is the … 'r', produced by turning the tip of the tongue back as far as possible into the hollow of the palate, and then imparting to the whole member as strong a vibration as it is capable of in this position. The result is a dull, deep vibrant sound, very different from the tip trill of a northern 'r' on the one hand, or the French and German 'r' on the other…'

which carries on for pages, suggesting a decidedly academic approach.

However, by way of illustration, he appends a translation of The Book of Ruth, beginning:
'Naew ut vaald aewt een dhai daiz, haun dhu jijez wuz u-rue-uleen…
(Now it came to pass in the days when the judges ruled…)'
with the comment that 'while being aware of the unsatisfactoriness of scripture specimens, this objection does not apply to a rural narrative like this book of the Bible.' Not so much a dry professor then, as an attentive listener to Exmoor speech, with a twinkle in his eye.

This sense of humour emerges in his many examples.

Thus, an abscess or tumour is called an *'apse'*:
'Her've got a apse 'pon her neck. This no doubt is an ignorant way of pronouncing *abscess*, which sounds so very like *aapsez*, and we all know that to be plural of *apse*. Inasmuch then as only one thing is referred to, we country folks naturally drop the plural inflection.'

He enjoyed a graffito in copper plate hand under a mirror:
'Things seen is Intempural
Things not seen is Inturnel'

And a labourer's comment on a concentrated manure – *'that there consecrated manure's double so good's the tother.'*

All of which highlights a key aspect of our local dialect – its humour.
A long tradition dates back at least to the eighteenth century, with 'Exmoor Courtship' and 'An Exmoor Scolding' – short dialogues in phonetic dialect for general entertainment – continuing through fictitious characters like Jarge Balsh, Dan'l Grainger and Jan Stewer into the twentieth.

Even when not being consciously humorous, it is naturally an attractive dialect.
Part of that distinctive singing quality arises from the agreeable burr – as with the already carefully described distinctive 'r'.
Then we have the dropped letters, especially 'h's. Almost mischievously, 'h's absent themselves, creating momentary confusion – 'head' turns into *'aid'*, 'home' into *'aum'*, and 'hundred' might become *'uun-durd'*. Meanwhile, they pop up where they should not be, with similar effect – *'haak-shulee'* is really 'actually', and *'haak-sedunt'* an accident. Other consonants also quietly drop out, especially 'b's and 'd's, as in *'bu'mm'l'*, *'an'l'* and *'nee'l'* for bumble, handle and needle respectively.
The stress on soft consonants, and the general elision make for a soft flavour. Thus Mrs Tudball's dictums as cited in earlier Reviews, even if intended more as Exmoor jokes than examples of the dialect:

'What's on wi' all they traffic?'
''Tis a weddin' at the Catholic church.'
'Don't hold wi' they. I bin a Strict Prostitute all me life.'

'Mr Damerel, that piece of meat you sold me las' wik was turr'ble tough.'
'Dammee, Missis, you mus' get tough with it.'

But of course it's more than accent, characteristic rhythms and cadences – there's the vocabulary which called for Elworthy's huge tome.
Sometimes words are only slight variations of Standard English, with a changed, more mellifluous consonant – *'vump'* (thump), or a dropped sound – *'vet'* (fetch), or altered vowels and diphthongs – *'upreart'* (upright), and *'crewnt'* (grunt or complain).

Some hark back to a more old fashioned, even archaic English, as in *'vorenoon'* (morning), *'furdle'*, meaning to fold up, *'hurn'* an Old English word for to run, and so on.

Others are plain onomatopoeic. *'Zwer'* is a whizzing noise, as of the sudden rise of a covey of partridges, *'lurruping'* meaning awkward, slouching furtively, and *'miz-maze'*…

'When I zeed the vire, I could'n do nothin, I was all to a miz-maze' said the woman, after her house was burnt.

It all adds up to an intriguing, indeed charming dialect. Which demonstrates the risk of enjoying any special way of speaking – we can only too easily turn from bemusement if not amusement, into slightly superior spectators, who find themselves smiling at this quaint form of speaking.

Is it possible to accept Coleman Cooke's challenge, to preserve and protect Exmoor speech as part of Exmoor's unique quality, without condescension, while acknowledging the reality of standardisation, which represents modern life?

Centralisation proceeds apace, whether we like it or not. With the homogenisation of language that television in particular reinforces, local ways of speaking are under threat.
On the other hand, no one would want the young people of Exmoor not to have access to all that today's educational system can offer, so that they do not have to become shepherds, unless of course that is their choice.

But, as with the landscape, we would all want to preserve those iconic features that make a place what it is: to recognise them, and if needs be, to protect them.

Happily, a renewed respect is now being given to local dialect and language. Cornish has been resurrected just in time, and more young people speak Welsh. Perhaps economic revival and prosperity hold the key to creating and maintaining confidence in our locality and what it stands for, with its unique and invaluable traditions and culture.

As with other aspects of Exmoor, we have to strike a balance between preservation and development.
Woe betide an England which has merged all into a standard uniformity. Almost worse would be a whole country increasingly like everywhere else. And language, what we hear, is as much a part of this, as what we see.

Good old Elworthy comes to our rescue.
Often when describing our local dialect, he compares it to what he calls 'ordinary English.' Perhaps we should therefore consider Exmoor dialect a form of English that is not so much ordinary, as special: we can all (more or less) speak English, but the particular English of our locality is something more. Matching the memorable and

distinctive landscape, this dialect has managed to survive – rich but gentle, subtle and characteristic, like the moor itself.

I hope – as I'm sure would Coleman Cooke – that we can share his confident prediction: 'Long experience has now convinced me… that our hereditary pronunciation will survive, together with our grammatical peculiarities, long after board schools and newspapers have brought English as a written language to one dead level.'

THE SOCIETY'S YEAR IN RETROSPECT

HIGHLIGHTS OF THE YEAR

- Successful outcome of the Public Inquiry into wind farms. Planning permission refused as the inspector decided that large industrial turbines just outside Exmoor would have a detrimental impact on the special qualities of the national park and its setting.

- Achieved the bid to Heritage Lottery Fund for the Moorland Landscape Partnership Scheme, based on recommendations from the Society's *"Moorlands at a Crossroads"* report.

- Continued hill farming campaign and drew attention to the complexities of agri-environmental schemes.

- Raised awareness of Exmoor's potential for providing renewable energy at a successful spring conference.

- Launched an educational endowment fund with donations of £6,500.

- Grants given to new woodlands, upland farming research, Dunster working group, Dulverton action plan to underground wires, perception study into Exmoor's landscapes and Exmoor Horn Sheep Breeders Society.

- Undertook a wide range of social activities including a well supported walks programme, a celebration picnic, farm and field visits.

GOVERNANCE

The Society continued its programme of delivering its aims and objectives, and running the charity efficiently. It has continued to influence policy matters by meetings with key public bodies, such as Exmoor National Park Authority (ENPA), Natural England (NE), Environment Agency (EA) and making its hopes and concerns known, often behind the scenes. It is represented on a number of local advisory groups and projects and is increasingly asked to give talks and have a presence at particular events. By using its website, press releases and media interviews, it has continued to raise the profile of national park status and the Society's role as a watchdog and champion for Exmoor.

The Executive has held five meetings and five policy ones in the year and has concentrated on securing different sources of funding so that the Society can increase its work. It has been even more successful this year in gaining sponsorship, raising money for specific projects and making special appeals. It continues to watch carefully its expenditure but with rising costs has had to make difficult decisions. Out of the subscription rate of £15 the Society returns a value of £8.50 which includes the spring newsletter, AGM mailing and the Exmoor Review in March, August and October respectively along with opportunities to attend a range of events, and of course the use of the Society's well-stocked library and archives.

The Society values its members and particularly does not want to lose any during these difficult economic times. It has decided not to put up its general subscriptions until 2011, but will this year appeal to members currently on concessionary rates asking them to increase them if possible. It continues to watch costs; for example, savings can be made on printing costs by not sending the Annual Report to individual members. It will be available at the AGM, in the Exmoor Review, on the website or, at the request of any member, sent by email or post. There will still be three mailings a year (despite increased postage costs).

TREASURER'S REPORT ON THE FINANCIAL ACCOUNTS FOR THE YEAR ENDED 31ST MAY 2010

This was another challenging financial year but it is pleasing to report that the overall balance sheet funds increased by £19,543. Total funds stood at £196,958 at the end of the financial year. This maintains our aim of providing the Society with financial stability in order to continue our aims and objectives.

Unrestricted funds are required to cover core costs including staffing and support and also to provide funds to be designated at short notice. This year the target was reached and overall a net increase in funds was achieved of £16,208 due an overall increase in investment assets and a revaluation of the library.

Investment income is included in the unrestricted funds and although the Society was not immune to the continued economic turmoil the COIF investment portfolio is continuing to steadily recover. The COIF funds stand at £93,564 (31st May 2010) an increase in value of nearly 11% from the previous year.

Restricted funds have increased by £3,335 maintaining our commitments to projects for the enhancement and awareness of Exmoor. The expenditure on the Public Inquiry into Wind Farms was completely justified by the refusal for planning permission and this is a wonderful example of our members digging deep into their pockets after our Chairman's appeal.

We are indebted to members for their contributions in the form of subscriptions, donations and legacies and we hope monies contributed can be quantified by the various highlights of the year detailed in "The Year in Retrospect".

However subscriptions will inevitably have to increase next year but the Executive hope that members realize their contributions are well utilized and supports a charity that acts as a strong guardian for Exmoor.

The trustees will continue to review all aspects of the Society's finances and maintain our policy of being acceptable and transparent to all our members.

INFLUENCING POLICY

There has been an unusually intense period of activity in major policy consultations, and the Society has responded to those that will have great impact on Exmoor.

Future of the English Uplands:
National attention on the plight of the English Uplands has led to the Society making robust responses to NE and the Commission for Rural Communities (CRC). The report 'High Ground, High Potential' from CRC supports most of the points made by the Society, such as the importance of hill farming practices in managing the landscape, of keeping stock on the moorlands and the need to retain the hill farming community through better rewards for the public goods they provide. The Society pressed NE to recognise clearly that the uplands are cultural landscapes and agri-environmental schemes need to be more tailored to local conditions, less bureaucratic and able to utilise local knowledge and skills. The Society continues to make these points at different forums and is part of a working group set up by NE to explore how farmers can be paid for the provision of eco-system services.

Management of Exmoor's Moorlands:
The Society has raised several issues with South West Uplands Task Force (SWUTF) and the ENPA in relation to moorland management. Although supporting the Mire Project in principle it has kept a watchful eye on its progress and raised several concerns about the implementation of the three year pilot project started in 2006. It was pleased to see that its lobbying has led to a review by South West Water before extending it to a second phase covering a much wider area. Hydrology, selection of drainage ditches, historic environment, biodiversity, landscape and access are all challenging areas that need to be resolved and the need for a stronger focus on monitoring, research, transparency and greater local involvement.

Renewable Energy:
The Society's spring conference in partnership with ENPA is an important event in the Exmoor calendar for raising important issues of the day. Held in April, it was successful in attracting a large audience to debate and to hear from practitioners the successes and failures of different renewable energy schemes. Exmoor has the opportunity to exploit a variety of sources ranging from biomass and hydro-electricity, solar and wind to developing community schemes across the moor, without harming the landscape and heritage assets.

A New National Park Circular:
Circulars have an important role in setting out Government policy and Defra decided this year to update the one for national parks. In response to a consultation the Society argued that it provided an opportunity for a clear statement on the

purposes of national parks and how NPAs should operate. One area of concern was a general misunderstanding of the NPA's role as environmental bodies and how they differed from Local Authorities (LA) responsible for a wider range of functions and still operating within the park boundaries. The Society recognised that the planning system through development control functions of the NPA can distort attention from their core work and help reinforce negative perceptions of local people. It argued that ENPA should be encouraged to experiment with delegating this function to district councils either by theme or area. The new circular puts greater emphasis on the core functions of NPAs, but still expects too much from them both in the bureaucracy involved and partnerships required with other public bodies.

Miscellaneous:
The Society has continued to influence a range of controversial matters within the park in relation to canoeing, the Lyn hydro-electric scheme, Anstey Common, Stone Lane and other Rights of Way improvements and swaling management. The Society responded to the ENPA's policy paper on swaling.

PARTNERSHIPS

Many projects depend on successful partnerships and the Society continues to recognise that it achieves more by working with others. The success of the wind farm campaign by forming the Exmoor Rural Alliance with CPRE and the Two Moors Campaign this year demonstrates the point clearly. The Society continues to work with SWUTF and its action programme for dealing with the problems of hill farming. It contributed financially to research work to find out the funding gap that hill farmers will face as a result of changes to CAP by 2012. The Exmoor Landscape Partnership bid to HLF has been successful and the Society has confirmed a financial contribution to the Landscape Project through a large donation for this particular purpose. The Landscape Advisory Group (LAG) continues to monitor the landscape section of the national park management plan. The Society has been grant-aided to commission a perception study as part of the objective to encourage people to celebrate and enjoy Exmoor's fine landscapes. Other partnerships include the Moorland Board, Dunster Working Group with financial support, Dulverton Action Plan with financial help to the undergrounding of wires, ENPAs consultative committee, access forum and sustainable development fund, and also the National Trust and South West Lakes Trust.

An important partnership includes the Society's Woodland Conservation Fund, the ENPA and the Forestry Commission (FC). The fund provides top up grants to small woodlands below 10 acres after application to the FC. Members of the Fund visited Horner Woods in October and in June looked at the condition of woodland that had been successfully planted several years ago with the aid of grants from the fund: Higher Gretton at Winsford, Lyshwell & Cloggs and Lord Plantation. There was a long discussion on the serious crisis caused by Phytophthora which is devastating and had spread to some Exmoor woodlands which had to be immediately felled.

PLANNING

Development Control:
The Society continues to monitor all planning applications, over 90% of which are decided under a scheme of delegation so do not come before the planning committee. It takes a pragmatic view on most applications coming to ENPA's Planning Committee, rarely objecting unless detrimental to landscape and amenity issues and against plan policies and sometimes raising concerns or asking for site visits to enable further considerations. All wind turbine applications are brought to the committee because of their impact on landscape. This year the Society has only objected to two; one at Exford because of amenity concerns and the other at Glenthorne because of the remarkable assemblage of conservation assets in that particular setting.

Local Development Framework:
The Society has continued its involvement in this long process by responding to consultation events and a stakeholder questionnaire.

Public Inquiry into Wind Farms:
The refusal of planning permission for two wind farms just outside the national park boundary was a major achievement. All the work the Society has done in setting up and chairing a Landscape Advisory Group and in persuading the ENPA to refocus on landscape matters in the National Park Management Plan and to undertake a more detailed landscape assessment and identify the parks special qualities has come to fruition. The inspector's reasons were clear: both wind farms would have had a detrimental impact on Exmoor's landscape, special qualities and setting.

EDUCATION, OUTREACH & AWARDS

The Society has continued to focus on its educational work by continuing to support Dulverton Middle School and the Exmoor Curriculum. It helped commission Plymouth University's Report on the Exmoor Curriculum and supported its recommendations to increase its links to subjects like Geography and History and to extend it to other schools within the Exmoor catchment.

An Educational Endowment Fund was launched in May at the Glenthorne Literary Museum by kind permission of Sir Christopher & Lady Ondaatje. It raised £6,500 in order to expand the Society's educational outreach and to fund children's literary and arts awards, as well as helping to extend the Exmoor Curriculum.

The environmental play "Tracks & Traces" has been extended to secondary schools through a further grant from the Sustainable Development Fund.

The bi-annual Alfred Vowles Photographic competition in January led to a large number of high quality photographs being submitted, with the winning entries reproduced here. An exhibition of them all at the Porlock Visitor Centre was well received.

A new award has been launched this year for adult poetry inspired by Exmoor. The winner will be announced at this year's AGM in September.

EVENTS

During the year over 50 events have been held for the membership and the wider public by the main Society and the Groups. The walks programme goes from strength to strength both in attendance and in the variety of themes: archaeology, mining and mystery, Lorna Doone, ancient Exmoor. The Christmas lunch at the Dunster Tithe Barn was a sell out and members were highly entertained by Tony Beard, the Wag of Widdicombe.

Warren Farm provided a magnificent setting hidden by the mist and rain for the annual farm visit, demonstrating the importance of integrating moorland with in-bye land and the farm system and business. Andrew Hawkins described how he has changed his farming system to fit with the environmental needs of the moorland. By changing from sheep to cattle he has been able to bring back more heather and other plants into the molinia areas. The complexities of managing the moorland, including livestock numbers and winter grazing, swaling and cutting the molinia, increased biodiversity were all discussed.

A surprise birthday celebration for the President, Sir Antony Acland, was well attended in June when members met at Webbers Post and walked to the Jubilee Hut. Much to his surprise, Sir Antony was asked to unveil a plaque to commemorate his 80th birthday. The National Trust provided a tea at Piles Mill to conclude the celebrations.

Congratulations were given to the Bristol Group on its 10th anniversary and on the way it contributed to the work of the Society, and most recently in sponsoring children from Bristol schools to spend a weekend at the Pinkery Education Centre. The Porlock Group supported the Forest Schools Initiative.

The Society continued to have a presence at three agricultural shows: Dunster Fair, Exford Show and Dunster Show. It is grateful to all the volunteers who look after the stands and help the Society in its work in so many other ways throughout the year. The Society also had a stand at its adopted church, St Luke's at Simonsbath during their celebration weekend at the beginning of July.

BIOGRAPHIES OF CONTRIBUTORS

S BAILEY
Sharon, who learnt about Exmoor from an early age on horseback, now lives at South Molton and photographs all aspects of rural life, including people.

H BINDING
Hilary is a recently retired teacher, local historian and writer. For some twenty years she was Editor of the Exmoor Review, and has written many books on Exmoor.

P CAREY
Phil settled here 15 years ago. He has a keen interest in the special qualities and history of the moor, and is a member of the Lyn Riparian Owners' Association.

J COX
Jeff is the great-great grandson of the printer Samuel Cox, who launched the *Free Press* in 1860. Jeff has been a journalist all his life, now working for BBC News.

J DE WYNTER-SMITH
A student at Dulverton Middle School, won first prize in the senior category of the Exmoor Society Writing Competition.

J DWYER
Janet is Professor of Rural Policy and Co-Director of the Countryside and Community Research Institute, a collaborative research unit of the Universities of Gloucestershire and the West of England, in partnership with The Royal Agricultural and Hartpury Colleges.

R FERRAR
A retired doctor, Roger still lives in Lynton, continuing to contribute to many aspects of Exmoor life, following the admirable example set by his fondly remembered colleague, Dr Mold.

B HAMILTON-BAILLIE
Ben is an architect, urban designer and movement specialist, whose work on behavioural psychology and the factors that promote civility has helped transform assumptions and practice concerning traffic and urban renewal.

S HEAD
A lecturer and consultant on environment sustainability, conservation, zoology, ecology and landscape history. Stephen is a Fellow of the Linnean Society and a Secretary of State appointed member of the Park Authority.

P KING-FRETTS
Paddy was brought up on the moor and, after many adventures including a distinguished military career, returned to his roots to write a much enjoyed Exmoor trilogy.

E MCLAUGHLIN
Elizabeth lives in the East Lyn Valley and is a Trustee and executive member of The Exmoor Society.

R MCLAUGHLIN
Richard is a chartered civil engineer, now retired and living near Brendon, but continues to advise the Army on technical and commercial matters. He chairs the

Exmoor National Park's panel on the award of sustainability grants.

E MORRISH
Emily was an eleven year old student at West Buckland School when she won first prize in the Junior category of the Exmoor society Writing competition.

T OLIVER
Tom, a landscape architect, was Head of Rural Policy at the Campaign to Protect Rural England. Before that, he worked for the Campaign for National Parks and the National Trust. He was brought up in South Molton where his father was Rector.

A PHILLIPS
Adrian was Director-General of the former Countryside Commission from 1981-1992. Since then he has held a portfolio of paid and voluntary positions, here and abroad, in the fields of conservation, landscape and environment.

F PRESLEY
Frances is a distinguished poet, frequently drawing on Exmoor in her work – as in *Stone Settings* – who has been inspired by Hazel Eardley-Wilmot.

S PUGSLEY
Steven is an Exmoor native and publisher. He sits on the Exmoor National Park authority and was its Chairman from 2001 to 2007.

D ROLLS
David is the Mosaic Youth Officer.

Growing up in Devon developed within him a passion for Exmoor National Park. Before joining the Mosaic team he was the Social Inclusion Manager at the Community Council of Devon.

N STONE
Chief Executive at Exmoor National Park Authority since October 1999.

C TAYLOR
Since 1989 Clare has been addressing diversity in the environmental movement. Prior to her post as Mosaic Project Officer, she worked as a youth social worker and psychological assistant in the prison service.

R THOMAS
Rachel is the Chair of the Exmoor Society.

A TIERNEY-JONES
Adrian is an award-winning freelance journalist based in Dulverton whose work appears in the *Daily Telegraph* (regular pub reviews and features on the countryside page), and in many other publications.

J WESTCOTT
Judith specialises in print making, particularly black and white linocuts, many of which have appeared in earlier Reviews.

R WILSON-NORTH
A Field Archaeologist, has been involved with Exmoor's historic landscape since 1993. He leads the Historic Environment team at Exmoor National Park Authority.